SPACE ODYSSEYS

ILLUSTRATED HISTORY OF THE FIRST 28 MISSIONS TO OUTER SPACE

By Gerald F. Pleau

T0353970

AuthorHouse™
1663 Liberty Drive
Bloomington, IN 47403
www.authorhouse.com
Phone: 1-800-839-8640

First published by AuthorHouse   5/13/2011

ISBN: 978-1-4567-2028-5 (sc)
ISBN: 978-1-4567-2027-8 (e)

Printed in the United States of America

Any people depicted in stock imagery provided by Thinkstock are models,
and such images are being used for illustrative purposes only.
Certain stock imagery © Thinkstock.

This book is printed on acid-free paper.

References to the source of information contained in this book were retrieved from the internet at: www.nasa.gov

This book is Dedicated to my Grandchildren: Leigh Ellen, Louis, Mickey, Autumn, Rachel, Maddison, and to all the children around the world. May this book encourage you to be everything God wants you to be, and inspire you to follow your dreams!

Acknowledgments

I would like to thank Roy Adcock Jr. for all his hard work in gathering this information together, and to everyone else who worked so hard in putting this book together.

I would also like to give a special thank you to my wife for all her love and encouragement during the past two years. Without whom this book would not be possible.

CONTENTS

President John F. Kennedy initiated the Apollo program amidst a tense Cold War political environment. In a speech to Congress on 25 May 1961, Kennedy outlined his Apollo program, a plan to send an American to the Moon by the end of the decade. This program, he hoped, would remind the world of American's enormous technical capability.

The Apollo program succeeded. On 20 July 1969, the world witnessed what was arguably the most astonishing technological achievement in history when Neil Armstrong and Edwin "Buzz" Aldrin became the first humans to set foot on the Moon. While Apollo 11 was an astounding technological, requiring the cooperation of many thousands of dedicated individuals.

Innovation and even improvisation were necessary along the way. In December 1968, rather than letting lunar module delays slow the program, NASA changed plans to keep the momentum going. Apollo 8 would go all the way to the moon and orbit without a lunar module; it was the first manned flight of the massive Saturn V rocket. Six of the missions- Apollo 11, 12, 14, 15, 16, and 17- went on to land on the moon.

APRIL 11, 1970

JANUARY 31, 1971

JUNE 26, 1971

APRIL 16, 1972

DECEMBER 7, 1972

DECEMBER 21, 1968

MARCH 3, 1969

MAY 18, 1969

JULY 16, 1969

NOVEMBER 14, 1969

JANUARY 27, 1967

OCTOBER 11, 1968

SEPTEMBER 12, 1966

NOVEMBER 11, 1966

JUNE 3, 1966

JULY 18, 1966

DECEMBER 15, 1965

MARCH 16, 1966

SPACE ODYSSEYS

MAY 15, 1963

MARCH 23, 1965

JUNE 3, 1965

AUGUST 21, 1965

DECEMBER 4, 1965

MAY 5, 1961

JULY 21, 1961

FEBRUARY 20, 1962

MAY 24, 1962

OCTOBER 3, 1962

GERALD PLEAU, INC. • 863.382.3962 •

Crew:

Alan B Shepard, Jr.

Mission Objective:

The main scientific objective of project **Mercury** was to determine man's capabilities in a space environment and returning from space. A few of the basic flight problems included: The development of an automatic escape system, vehicle control during insertion, behavior of space systems, evaluation of pilots capabilities in space, in flight monitoring, retrofire and reentry maneuvers and landing and recovery.

1

Launch:

May 5, 1961 9:34 am EST.

Orbit:

Altitude: 116.5 statute miles
Orbits: 0
Duration: 0 Days, 0 hours, 15 min, 28 seconds
Distance: 303 statute miles
Velocity: 5,134 mph

Landing:

May 5, 1961. 75 deg 53 min longitude, 27 deg 13.7 min latitude in the
Atlantic Ocean.

Mission Highlights:

Mission was successful.

MERCURY 3

1. What President of the United States along with NASA started the space program?

2. Who was the first astronaut to go into space?

3. When was Mercury 3 launched?

4. What was the duration of the launch?

5. How many miles did the Mercury travel?

6. What was the mission objective?

7. What was the mission highlights?

Crew:

Virgil I "Gus" Grissom

Backup Crew:

John H. Glenn, Jr.

Mission Objective:

Mercury Redstone 4 was the fourth mission in the Mercury – Redstone series of flight tests and the second U.S. manned suborbital spaceflight. It was the next step in the progressive research, development and training program leading to the study of man's capabilities in a space environment during manned orbital flight. The main objective was to corroborate the man-in-space concept. The main configuration differences between the MR-3 spacecraft were the addition of a large viewing window and an explosively actuated side hatch. The addition of the large viewing window was the result of a change requested by Mercury astronauts. This window allowed the astronauts to have a greater viewing area than the original side port windows. The field of view was 30 degrees in the horizontal plane and 33

1

degrees in the vertical. The window is composed of an outer panel of 0.35-inch thick Vycor glass and a 3-layer inner panel.

The explosively actuated side hatch was used for the first time on the MR-4 fight. The mechanically operated side hatch on the MR-3 spacecraft was in the same location and of the same size but was considerably heavier (69 pounds rather than 23 pounds). The explosively actuated hatch utilizes an explosive charge to fracture the attaching bolts and thus separated the hatch from the spacecraft. Seventy ¼ inch titanium bolts secure the hatch to the doorsill. A 0.06- inch diameter hole is drilled in each bolt to provide a weak point. A mild detonating fuse (MDF) is installed in a channel between an inner and outer seal around the periphery of the hatch. When the MDF is ignited, the resulting gas pressure between the inner and outer seal causes the bolts to fail in tension. The MDF is ignited by a manually operated igniter that requires an actuation force of around 5 pounds, after the removal of a safety pin. The igniter can be operated externally by an attached lanyard, in which case a force of at least 40 pounds is required in order to shear the safety pin.

Launch:

July 21, 1961. 7: 20 a.m. EST. The launch was originally scheduled for July 18, 1961 but was rescheduled to July 19, 1961 because of unfavorable weather conditions. The launch attempt on July 19, 1961 was canceled at T-10 as a result of continued unfavorable weather. The launch was then rescheduled for July 21, 1961. The first half of the split launch was then rescheduled for EST on July 20, 1961 at T-640 minutes. Spacecraft preparation proceeded normally thru the 12-hour planned hold period for hydrogen peroxide and pyrotechnic servicing. Evaluation of the weather at this time proved favorable and a go was given to pick up the second half of the countdown at 2:30a.m. EST on July 20, 1961. At T-180 minutes, prior to liquid oxygen loading, a planned 1-hour hold was called for another weather evaluation. The evaluation was favorable and the count proceeded at 3:00a.m EST. At T-45 minutes a 30 minute hold was called to install a misaligned hatch bolt. At T-30 minutes, a 9 minute hold was called to turn off the pad searchlights which interfered with launch telemetry during launch. At T-15 minutes, a 41 minute hold was called to await better cloud conditions. The count proceeded from T-15 until liftoff. Gus Grissom was in the spacecraft 3 hours and 22 minutes prior to launch.

The spacecraft was delivered to Hanger S at Cape Canaveral, Florida on March 7, 1961. Upon delivery, the instrumentation and selected items of the communication system were removed from the spacecraft for bench testing. After reinstallation of the components, the systems test proceeded as scheduled. Those tests required a total of 33 days during which the electrical, sequential, instrumentation, communication, environmental, reaction-control, and stabilization and control systems were individually tested. After system tests, the landing impact bag was installed and then a simulated flight was run on the spacecraft. Then the parachutes and pyrotechnics were installed and the spacecraft was weighed, balanced and then delivered to the launch complex. Twenty-one days were spent on the launch pad.

Orbit

Altitude: 118.3 statute miles
Orbits: 0
Duration: 0 Days, 0 hours, 15 min, 37 seconds
Distance: 302 statute miles
Velocity: 5,134 mph

Landing:

In the Atlantic Ocean, which was 302 miles east of launch site? Drogue parachute was deployed at T+9 minutes 41 seconds and main parachute at T+10 minutes 14 seconds. Landing occurred at T+15 minutes 37 seconds.

Mission Highlights:

The MR-4 flight plan was very much the same as that for MR-3. The range was 262.5 nautical miles, the maximum altitude was 102.8 nautical miles, and the period of weightlessness lasted for approximately 5 minutes.

At T-35 seconds, the spacecraft umbilical was pulled and the periscope was retracted. During the boosted phase of flight, the flight-path angle was controlled by the launch-vehicle control system. Launch-vehicle cutoff occurred at T+2 minutes 23 seconds, at which time the escape tower was released by firing the escape and tower jettison rockets. Ten seconds later, the spacecraft-to-launch-vehicle adapter clamp ring was separated, and the posigrade rockets fired to separate the spacecraft from the launch vehicle. The periscope was extended; the automatic stabilization and control system provided 5 seconds of rate damping, followed by spacecraft turnaround. It then oriented the spacecraft to orbit attitude of -34 degrees.

Retro sequence was initiated by timer at T+4 minutes 46 seconds, which was 30 seconds prior to the spacecraft reaching its apogee. Gus Grissom assumed control of the spacecraft attitude at T+3 minutes 5 seconds and controlled the spacecraft by the manual proportional control system to T+5 minutes 43seconds. He initiated firing of the retrorockets at T+5 minutes 10 seconds. From T+5 minutes 43 seconds, he controlled the spacecraft by the manual rate command system through reentry. The retrorocket package was jettisoned at T+6 minutes 7 seconds. The drogue parachute was deployed at T+9 minutes 41 seconds, and main parachute, at T+10 minutes 14 seconds. Landing occurred and flight successful but the spacecraft was lost during the post landing recovery period as a result of premature actuation of the explosively actuated side egress hatch. The capsule sank in 15,000 feet of water shortly after splashdown. The astronaut egressed from the spacecraft immediately after hatch actuation was retrieved after being in the water for about 3 to 4 minutes.

Mercury 4

1. When was the Mercury 4 launch into space?

2. Who were the crew members on the Mercury 4 mission?

3. Named the members of the backup crew for the Mercury 4 mission?

4. What was the duration time off this mission?

5. What were the main configuration differences between the MR-3 spacecraft and the MR-4 spacecraft?

6. What was this mission's objective?

7. What were this mission's highlights?

Crew:

John H. Glenn, Jr.

Mission Objective:

Place a man into earth orbit, observe his reactions to the space environment and safely return to earth to a point where he could be readily found. The Mercury flight plan during the first orbit was to maintain optimum spacecraft attitude for radar tracking and communication checks.

1

Launch:

February 20, 1962. 9:47: 39 a.m. EST. Cape Canaveral launches complex 14. Powered flight lasted 5 minutes 1 second and was completed normally. The Mercury countdown began on January 27, 1962 and was performed in two parts. Precount checks out the primary spacecraft systems, followed by a 17.5 hour hold for pyrotechnic checks, electrical connections and peroxide system servicing. Then the countdown began. The launch countdown proceeded to the T-13 minute mark and then was canceled due to adverse weather conditions. After cancellation, the mission team decided to replace the carbon dioxide absorber unit and the peroxide system had to be drained and flushed to prevent corrosion. Launch vehicle systems were then revalidated and a leak was discovered in the inner bulkhead of the fuel tank that required 4-6 days to repair. The launch was rescheduled to February 13, 1962 and then to February 14, 1962 to all the bulkhead work to complete. The precount picked up again on 2/13/62, 2/15/62 and then to 2/16/62 but was canceled each time due to adverse weather. The launch was then rescheduled for February 20, 1962. During the launch countdown on February 20, 1962, all systems were energized and final overall checks were made. The count started at T-390 minutes by installing and connecting the escape-rocket igniter. The service structure was then cleared and the spacecraft was powered to verify no inadvertent pyrotechnic ignition. The personnel then returned to service structure to prepare for static firing of the reaction control system at T-250 minutes.

The spacecraft was then prepared for boarding at T-120 minutes. The hatch was put into place at T-90 minutes. During installation a bolt was broken, and the hatch had to be removed to replace the bolt causing a 40 minute hold. From T-90 to T-55 final mechanical work and spacecraft checks were made and the service was evacuated and moved away from the launch vehicle. At T-45 minutes, a 15 minute hold was required to add fuel to the launch vehicle and at T-22 minutes and additional 25 minutes was required for filling the liquid-oxygen tanks as a result of a minor malfunction in the ground support equipment used to pump liquid oxygen into the launch vehicle. At approximately T-35 minutes, filling of the liquid-oxygen tanks began and final spacecraft and launch vehicle systems checks were started.

At T-10 minutes the spacecraft went on internal power. At T-6 min 30 seconds, a 2 minute hold was required to make a quick check of the network computer at Bermuda. The launch vehicle went on internal power at T-3 minutes. At T-35 seconds the spacecraft umbilical was ejected and at T-0 the main engines started. Liftoff occurred at T+4 seconds at 9:47:39 a.m. EST.

Orbit:

Altitude: 162.2x100 statute miles
Orbits: 3
Duration: 0 Days, 4 hours, 55 min, 23 seconds
Distance: 75,679 statute miles
Velocity: 17,544 mph

Landing:

February 20, 1962. 14:43:02 a.m. EST. 800 miles southeast of Bermuda. The mission was recovered by the destroyer by the destroyer USS Noa. Lookouts on the destroyer sighted the main parachute at an altitude of 5,000 ft from a range of 5nm. The Noa had the spacecraft aboard 21 minutes after landing and astronaut John Glenn remained in the spacecraft during pickup. Original plans had called for egress through the top hatch but Glenn was becoming uncomfortably warm and it was decided to exit by the easier egress path.

Mission Highlights:

Mission was successful. The MA-6 crew was the first Americans in orbit. The total time weightless was 4 hours 48 min 27seconds. During the flight only two major problems were encountered: (1) a yaw attitude control jet apparently clogged at the end of the first orbit, forcing the astronaut to abandon the automatic control system for the manual-electrical fly-by-wire system; and (2) a faulty switch in the heat shield circuit indicated that the clamp holding the shield had been prematurely released a signal later found to be false. During reentry, however, the retro pack was not jettisoned but retained as a safety measure to hold the heat shield in place in the event it had loosened.

Mercury Atlas 6

1. Who were the crew members of the MA-6?

2. What was the launch date of this mission?

3. The duration time of this mission was?

4. Can you name the backup crew members of the MA-6?

5. How many orbits did the MA-6 have?

6. What was the distance in miles that this mission traveled?

7. The speed of the spacecraft was?

8. What was the speed difference from the MR-4and the MA-6

9. The mission objective of this mission was?

10. What was the landing date of the MA-6?

11. Can you list these missions' highlights?

Crew:

M. Scott Carpenter

Mission Objective:

Corroborate man-in orbit.

Launch:

May 24, 1962. 7:45: 16 EST. The launch countdown proceeded almost perfectly, with only a last- minute hold of 45 minutes occurring at the T-11 minutes mark in anticipation of better camera coverage and to allow aircraft to check the atmospheric refraction index in the vicinity of Cape Canaveral. The launch vehicle used to accelerate Carpenter and the Aurora 7 spacecraft was an Atlas D. The differences between the Atlas 107-D launch vehicle and the Atlas 109-D used for MA-6 involved retention of the insulation bulkhead and reduction of the staging time from 131.3 to 130.1 seconds after liftoff. The performance of the launch vehicle was exceptionally good with the countdown, launch and insertion conforming very closely to planned conditions. At sustainer engine cutoff (SECO) at T+5 minutes 10 seconds, all spacecraft and launch vehicle systems were go and only one anomaly occurred during launch. The abort sensing and implementation system (ASIS) Hydraulic switch No. 2 for the sustainer engine actuated to the abort position at 4:25 minutes after liftoff. Pressure transducer H52P for the sustainer hydraulic accumulator was apparently faulty and showed a gradual decrease in pressure from 2,940 Pisa to 0 between 190 and 312 seconds after liftoff. Another transducer in the sustainer control circuit indicated that normal time after SECO.

Orbit:

Altitude: 166.8 by 99.9 statute miles
Orbits: 3
Duration: 0 Days, 4 hours, 56 min, 5 seconds
Distance: 76,021 statute miles
Velocity: 17,549 mph

Landing:

May 24, 1962. 12: 41p.m. EST. It landed 19degrees 29minutes North 64degrees 5minutes West. The spacecraft overshot the intended target area by 250 nautical miles. After landing, Carpenter reported a severe list angle on the order of 60 degrees from vertical and post flight photographs of the spacecraft taken after egress indicated approximately a 45 degree list angle. An Air Rescue Service SA-16 amphibian aircraft established visual contact with the spacecraft 39 minutes after landing (1:20p.m.) and the USS Farragut, located about 90 nautical miles southwest of the calculated landing position was first to reach the capsule.

Carpenter was picked up by HSS-2 helicopters dispatched from the aircraft carrier USS Intrepid (CVS-11) while the destroyer USS Farragut (DLG-6) watched the Aurora 7 capsule until it could be retrieved with special equipment aboard the USS John R. Pierce about 6 hours later. A considerable amount of sea water was found in the spacecraft which was believed to have entered through the small pressure bulkhead when Carpenter passed through the recovery compartment into the life raft. The spacecraft was delivered by destroyer to Roosevelt Roads, Puerto Rico with subsequent return to Cape Canaveral by airplane.

Mission Highlights:

Total time weightless was 4 hours 39 min 32 seconds. The performance of the Mercury spacecraft and Atlas launch vehicle was excellent in nearly every respect. All primary mission objectives were achieved. The single mission malfunction was due to a failure in the spacecraft pitch horizon scanner, which was a component of the automatic control system. This anomaly was adequately compensated for by the pilot in subsequent in flight operations so that the success of the mission was not compromised. A modification of the spacecraft control system thrust units was effective. Cabin and pressure-suit temperatures were high but not intolerable. Some uncertainties in the data telemeter from the bioinstrumentation prevailed at times during the flight; however, associated information; notably that regarding liquid behavior in a weightless state, identification of the airglow layer observed by Astronaut Glenn, and photography of terrestrial features and meteorological phenomena. An experiment which was to provide atmospheric drag and color visibility data in space through deployment of an inflatable sphere was partially successful. The flight further qualified the Mercury spacecraft systems for manned orbital operations and provided evidence for progressing into missions of extended duration and consequently more demanding systems requirements.

Mercury Atlas 7

1. On what date was the MA-7 launch?

2. What were the names of the crew members on this mission?

3. The duration of time for this mission was how long?

4. How many orbits did the MA-7 have?

5. On what date did the MA-7 land?

6. Where did the Mercury -7 Land?

7. What was the name of the ship that was the first to reach the capsule?

8. How long did it take to load the capsule aboard the USS John R. Pierce?

9. What were the mission objectives?

10. The mission highlights for the MA-7 were?

Crew:

Wally Schirra (was a member of the Ancient Order of Turtles).

Backup Crew:

Gordon Cooper

Launch:

October 3, 1962. 12:15: 11 p.m. UTC at Cape Canaveral Complex 14.

Orbit:

Orbits: 6
Duration: 9 hours, 13min 11seconds
Distance: 143,983 miles
Velocity: 17,558 mph

Landing:

October 3, 1962 21:28:22 UTC. The spacecraft landed 32 degrees 7' 30" N – 174 degrees 45' W. Midway Island Pacific.

Mission Highlights:

The Mercury Atlas 8 was a Mercury program manned space launched on October 3, 1962. The spacecraft was named Sigma 7 and completed six earth orbits piloted by astronaut Wally Schirra. It was the first flawless Mercury mission.

Schirra's was the first of two longer-duration Mercury missions. After Carpenter's flawed reentry, the emphasis returned to engineering rather than science (Schirra even named his spacecraft "Sigma" for the engineering symbol meaning "summation".) The six-orbit mission lasted 9 hours and 13minutes, much of which Schirra spent in what he called "chimp configuration," a free drift that tested the Mercury's autopilot system. Schirra also tried "steering" by the stars (he found this difficult), took photographs with a Hasselblad camera, exercised with a bungee cord device, saw lightning in the atmosphere, broadcast the first live message from an American spacecraft to radio and TV listeners below, and made the first splashdown in the Pacific. This was the highest flight of the Mercury program, with an apogee of 283.24km (176mi), but Schirra later claimed to be unimpressed with space scenery as compared to the view from high-flying aircraft. "Some old deal, nothing new," he told debriefers after the flight. Sigma 7 landed near the international date line in the Pacific Ocean, 275 miles (440 km) NE of Midway Island. The landing coordinates were near 32degrees 7' 30" North – 174 degrees 45' West.

The Mercury spacecraft #16 – Sigma 7, used in the Mercury-Atlas 8 mission, is currently displayed at the United States Astronaut Hall of Fame, Titusville, Florida.

Figure 1: The Mercury 8 space capsule is towed toward the USS Kearsarge for pickup after its orbital flight with astronaut "Wally" Schirra on board. Note the presence of the rescue swimmer on the capsule's flotation collar, and a Kearsarge 26-foot motor whaleboat standing by.

Figure2: Mercury 8 in its hangar.

Mercury Atlas-8

1. What were the names of the MA-8 crew members?

2. On what date was the MA-8 launched?

3. How many numbers of orbits did the MA-8 have?

4. The duration of this mission was how long?

5. What was the distance traveled by the MA-8?

6. On what day did the Mercury Atlas 8 land?

7. What was the name of the Island near where the MA-8 landed?

8. Can you name the members of the backup crew?

9. Wally Schirra revealed his membership to what organization?

10. What was some of this mission highlights?

Crew:

Gordon Cooper

Backup Crew:

Alan B. Shepard

Launch:

May 15, 1963. 13:04:13 UTC. It launched from Cape Canaveral Complex 14.

Orbit:

Orbits: 22
Duration: 34 hours 19 minutes 49 seconds
Distance: 546,167 statute miles
Velocity: 17,547 mph

Landing:

May 16, 1963. 23:23:02 UTC. It landed 27 degrees 30' north, 176 degrees 15' west Midway Island Pacific.

Flight Directors:

Chris Kraft. Red team
John Hodge. Blue team

Mission Highlights:

Mercury 9 was the last U.S. Mercury spaceflight manned space mission, launch on May 15, 1963 from Launch complex 14 at Cape Canaveral, Florida. The capsule was named Faith 7 and it completed 22 Earth orbits piloted by astronaut Gordon Cooper. The Atlas rocket was #130-D, and the Mercury spacecraft was #20.

The flight of Sigma 7 had been so nearly perfect that some thought America should quit while it was ahead and make MA-8 the last Mercury mission, and not risk the change of future disaster. They thought NASA had pushed the first- generation Mercury hardware far enough, and taking more chances on another longer mission were not warranted. They thought it was time to move on to the Gemini program.

Manned Spacecraft Center officials, however, believed that the Mercury team should be given the chance to test man in space for a full day. In addition, all of the Soviet single-seat Vostok spacecraft launched after Vostok 1 lasted for more than a day, thus the Mercury 9 flight would bring the Mercury spacecraft up to the same level as that of the Soviet.

In September, 1962, NASA concluded negotiations with McDonnell to modify four Mercury spacecraft (#12, #15, #17 and#20) to a configuration that supported a one-day mission.

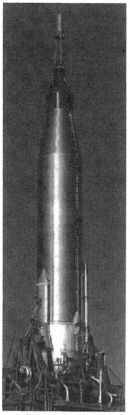

MA-9 launch

In November, 1962, Gordon Cooper was chosen to pilot the MA-9 mission and Alan Shepard was picked as backup.

On April 22, 1963 Atlas booster 130-D and Mercury spacecraft #20 were stacked on the launch pad at Launch Complex 14.

Because MA-9 would orbit over nearly every part of the world from 32.5 degrees north to 32.5 degrees south, a total of 28 ships, 171 aircrafts, and 18,000 servicemen were assigned to this mission.

 When Cooper boarded Faith 7 at 6:36 a.m. on the morning of May 4, he found a little gift that had been left for him. Alan Shepard had left behind a toilet plunger as a joke. Instructions on the handle said, "Remove before Launch". The gift didn't make the trip. Neither did Cooper that day. Various problems with radar in Bermuda and the diesel engine that rolls back the gantry caused the launch to be cancelled until May 15.

At 8:00:13 a.m. EST. May 15, 1963, Faith 7 was launched from Launch Complex 14. At T+60 seconds, the Atlas started its pitch program. Shortly afterward, MA-9 passed through Max-Q. At T+2 minutes and 14 seconds Cooper felt BECO (Booster Engine Cutoff) and staging. The two Atlas booster engines had been left behind. The Launch Escape Tower was then jettisoned. At T+3 minutes the cabin pressure sealed at 5.5 lb/in (38kPa). Cooper reported, "Faith 7 is all go."

At about T+5 minutes was SECO (Sustainer Engine Cutoff) and Faith 7 entered orbit at 17,547 mile/h (7,844 m/s). After the spacecraft separated and turned around to orbit attitude, Cooper watched his Atlas booster lag behind and tumble for about eight minutes. Over Zanzibar on the first orbit, he learned that the orbital parameters were good enough for at least 20 orbits. As the spacecraft passed over Guaymas, Mexico still on the first orbit, capsule communicator Gus Grissom told Cooper the ground computers said he was 'go for seven orbits".

At the start of the third orbit, Cooper checked his list of 11 experiments that were on his schedule. His first task was to eject a six-inch (152mm) diameter sphere, equipped with xenon strobe lights from the nose of the spacecraft. This experiment was designed to test his ability to sport and track a flashing beacon in orbit. At T+3 hours 25 minutes, Cooper flipped the switch and heard and felt the beacon detach from the spacecraft. He tried to see the flashing light in the approaching dusk and on the night side pass, but fail to do so. On the fourth orbit, he did spot the beacon and saw it pulsing. Cooper reported to Scott Carpenter on Kauai, Hawaii, "I was with the little rascal all night." He also spotted the beacon on his fifth and sixth orbits.

Also on the sixth orbit, at about T+9 hours, Cooper set up cameras, adjusted the spacecraft attitude and set switches to deploy a tethered balloon from the nose of the spacecraft. It was a 30 inch (762mm) PET film balloon painted fluorescent orange, inflated with nitrogen and attached to a 100 ft (30m) nylon line from the antenna canister. A strain gauge in the antenna canister would measure differences in atmospheric drag between the 100 mile (160km) perigee and the 160 mile (260km) apogee. Cooper tried several times to eject the balloon, but failed to eject.

Cooper passed Schirra's orbital recoT+10 hours; the Zanzibar tracking station informed Cooper the flight was a go for 17 orbits. Cooper was orbiting the earth every 88 minutes 45 seconds at an inclination of 32.55 degrees to the equator.

His scheduled rest period was during orbit 9 through 13. He had a dinner of powered roast beef mush and some water, took pictures of Asia and reported the spacecraft condition. Cooper was not sleepy and during orbit 9 took some of the best photos made during his flight. He took pictures of the Tibetan highlands and of the Himalayas.

Picture of Tibet taken by Cooper

He said he could see roads, rivers, small villages, and even individual houses if the lighting and background conditions were right. Cooper slept intermittently the next six hours, during orbits 10 through 13. He woke from time to time and took more pictures, taped status reports and kept adjusting his spacesuit temperature control which kept getting too hot or too cold.

On his fourteenth orbit, Cooper took an assessment of spacecraft condition. The oxygen supply was sufficient. The peroxide fuel for attitude control was 69 percent in the automatic tank and 95 percent in the manual one. On the fifteenth orbit, he spent most of the time calibrating equipment and synchronizing clocks.

When he entered night on the sixteenth orbit, Cooper pitched the spacecraft to slowly follow the plane of the ecliptic. Through the spacecraft window he viewed the zodiacal light and night airglow layer. He took pictures of these two "dim light" phenomena from Zanzibar, across the earth's night side, to

Canton Island. The pictures were later found to have been overexposed, but they still contained valuable data.

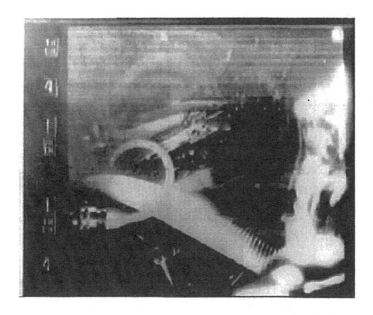

Astronaut Cooper's face and oxygen hose are visible in this b&w, slow scan TV picture taken on the 17th orbit and sent back to earth.

At the start of the 17th orbit while crossing Cape Canaveral, Florida, Cooper Broadcast slow scan black and white television picture to the ground. The picture showed a ghostly image of the astronaut. In the murky picture, a helmet and hoses could be seen; it was the first time an American astronaut had sent back television images from space.

On the 17th and 18th orbits, he took infrared weather photos moonset Earth limb pictures. He also resumed Geiger counter measurements of radiation. He sang during orbits 18 and19, and marveled at the greenery of Earth. It was nearing T+30 hours since liftoff.

On the nineteenth orbit, the first sign of trouble appeared when the spacecraft 0.05 g light came on. The spacecraft was not reentering, it was a faulty indicator. On the 20th orbit, Cooper lost all attitude readings. The 21st orbit saw a short circuit occur in the bus bar serving the 250 volt main inverter. This left the automatic stabilization and control system without electric power.

On the 21st orbit, John Glenn onboard the Coastal Sentry Quebec near Kyushu, Japan, helped Cooper prepared a revised checklist for retrofire. Due to the system malfunctions, many of the steps would have to be done manually. Only Hawaii and Zanzibar were in radio range on his last orbit, but communications were good. Cooper noted that the carbon dioxide level was rising in the cabin and in his spacesuit. He told Carpenter as he passed over Zanzibar, "Things are beginning to stack up a little." Throughout the problems, Cooper remained cool, calm and collected.

At the end of the 21st orbit, Cooper again contacted Glenn on the Coastal Sentry Quebec. He reported the spacecraft was in retro attitude and holding manually. Glenn gave a ten second countdown to retrofire. Cooper kept the spacecraft aligned at a 34 degree pitch down angle and manually fired the retrorockets on "Mark!"

On the flight deck of USS Kearsarge the crew spelled out "Mercury 9", while underway to recovery area.

Fifteen minutes later the faith 7 landed just four miles (6km) from the prime recovery ship, the carrier USS Kearsarge. The landing spot was just 130km south east of Midway Island, in the Pacific Ocean. This is south west of Pearl and Hermes Reef. The Mercury Project Summary Including Results of the Fourth Manned Orbital Flight, Faith 7 landed 70 nautical miles (130km) south east of Midway Island. This would be near 27 degrees 30' North, 176 degrees 15' West.

Splashdown was T+34 hours 19 minutes 49 seconds after liftoff. The spacecraft tipped over in the water momentarily, then righted itself. Helicopters dropped rescue swimmers and relayed Cooper's request of an Air Force officer, for permission to be hoisted aboard the Navy's carrier. Permission was granted, 40 minutes later the explosive hatch blew open on the deck of the Kearsarge. Cooper stepped out of the Faith 7 to a warm greeting.

After the MA-9 mission, there was another debate to fly one more Mercury flight, Mercury Atlas-10 (MA-10). It was proposed as a three day, 48 orbit missions to be flown by Alan Shepard in October 1963. In the end, officials decided it was time to move on to Project Gemini and MA-10 never flew.

The Mercury program had fulfilled all of its goals.

Capsule location:

The Faith 7 capsule is currently displayed at Space Center Houston, Houston, TX.

Mercury Atlas 9

1. Who were the crew members on the MA-9 mission?

2. Can you name the backup crew members?

3. How many orbits did the MA-9 mission have?

4. What was the distance the MA-9 traveled?

5. Who were the flight directors on the MA-9 mission?

6. When was the MA-9 launched?

7. The duration time of the MA-9 mission was?

8. Where is the Faith7 capsule displayed?

9. What happened to the (MA-10) mission?

10. Did the Mercury program fulfill all of its goals?

11. What were the mission high lights of this mission?

12. What gift did Alan Shepard leave for Gordon Cooper?

13. The instructions written on the gift were what?

Crew:

    Virgil I. Grissom- commander

    John W. Young- pilot

Backup Crew:

    Walter M. Schirra Jr.

    Thomas P. Stafford

Launch:

    On March 23, 1965 at 9:24:00.064 a.m. EST. the Gemini 3 was launched

Orbit:

    Altitude: 224km
    Orbits: 3
    Duration: 0 days 4 hours 52 minutes 31 seconds
    Distance: 128,748 km

Landing:

    March 23, 1965.

Mission Objective:

Demonstrate manned orbital flight; evaluate two-man design. Demonstrate and evaluate tracking network. Demonstrate OAMS capability in orbital maneuvers and in retrofire backup. Demonstrate controlled reentry and landing. Evaluate major spacecraft subsystems. Demonstrate systems checkout, prelaunch, and launch procedures. Demonstrate and evaluate recovery procedures and systems Spacecraft weight 3225kg

Secondary objectives included: evaluate flight crew equipment, biomedical instrumentation, and personal hygiene system. Perform 3 experiments. Evaluate low-level longitudinal oscillations (Pogo) of the GLV, General photographic coverage in orbit.

Mission Highlights:

All primary objectives were achieved except the controlled reentry objective was only partially achieved. The angle of attack during reentry was lower than expected. Secondary objectives were only partially achieved. The personal hygiene system was only partially tested; operating mechanism failed on S-2 Synergistic Effect of Zero Gravity on Sea Urchin Eggs Experiment and the photographic coverage objective was only partially successful because of an improper lens setting on the 16mm camera. There was one brief hold on launch day while a sensor on an oxidizer line was adjusted. Landing on March 23, 1965 was at 22 degrees 26m north and 70 degrees 51min west. The Gemini 3 missed distance from landing zone 111.1km (60nm).It was recovered by the USS Intrepid

Gemini 3

1. Who were the crew members on the Gemini 3 mission?

2. Can you name the backup crew members for this mission?

3. What was the orbit altitude?

4. The duration time of this mission was?

5. When was the Gemini-3 mission launched?

6. The Gemini-3 mission landed on date?

7. Where did this mission land?

8. What were the objectives of this mission?

9. How many orbits did the Gemini-3 mission have?

10. The mission highlights were?

Crew:

      James A. McDivitt - commander
      Edward H. White II – Pilot

Backup crew:
      Frank Borman
      James A. Lovell, Jr.

Mission Objective:
      Evaluate effects of prolonged space flight. Demonstrate and evaluate
      performance of spacecraft and systems in 4 day flight Evaluate procedures

for crew rest and work cycles, eating schedules, and real time flight planning. Spacecraft weight: 3574kg.

Secondary objectives included: demonstrate evaluate EVA and control by use of HHMU and tether. Station keep and rendezvous with second stage of GLV. Evaluate spacecraft systems. Make in-and-out-of plane maneuvers. Further test OAMS retro backup capability. They performed 11 experiments.

Launch:

On June 3, 1965 at 10:15:59.562 am

Orbit:

Altitude: 296.1 km
Orbits: 62
Duration: 4 days, 1hour, 56minutes, 12 seconds

Landing:

June 7, 1965. Landing was at 27 degrees 44min north and 74 degrees 11min west. Landing was 81.4km from attempted landing zone.

Mission Highlights:

Gemini 4 was the space programs 1st Extra Vehicular Activity (EVA) operation. EVA time 36 minutes.

All but one primary objective was achieved. Computer controlled reentry in the demonstration and evaluation of spacecraft systems objective was not flown because of inadvertent alteration of computer memory. All secondary objectives were met except one. The secondary objective of station keeping and rendezvous was only partially successful because separation and rendezvous was not attempted due to fuel consumption.

Gemini 4

1. Who were the crew members on the Gemini 4 mission?

2. Can you name the members of the backup crew for this mission?

3. What were the mission objectives for the Gemini 4 mission?

4. When was the Gemini 4 launched?

5. What was the duration of this mission?

6. How many orbits did this mission have?

7. When did the Gemini 4 land?

8. Did the Gemini 4 land at the attempted landing zone?

9. What were the highlights of this mission?

10. Did this mission achieve all its objectives?

Crew:

C. Gordon Cooper Commander
Charles Conrad, Jr. Pilot

Backup Crew:

Neil A. Armstrong
Elliot M. See, Jr.

Mission Objective:

Evaluate rendezvous Guidance and Navigation system with REP. Demonstrate 8 day capability of spacecraft and crew. Evaluate effects on weightlessness for 8 day flight. Spacecraft weight: 360kg.

Secondary objectives included: Demonstrate controlled reentry guidance. Evaluate fuel cell. Demonstrate all phases of guidance and control system operation needed for rendezvous. Checkout rendezvous radar. Execute 17 experiments.

Launch:

August 21, 1965; 8:59:.518a.m EST. A launch attempt on August 19 was postponed due to weather conditions and problems with loading cryogenic fuel for the fuel cell.

Orbit:

Altitude: 349.8km
Orbits: 120
Duration: 7days, 22hours, 55minutes, 14seconds

Landing:

August 29, 1965. Landing was at 29 deg44min north and 69deg 45min west. Miss distance was 170.3km. Navy divers from the backup recovery ship USS DuPont (DD-941) recovered the crew and transferred them via helicopter to the USS Lake Champlain (crew onboard in 89 min).

Mission Highlights:

During the mission, problems developed with the fuel cell that precluded rendezvous with the radar evaluation pod (REP). Primary rendezvous G&N system with REP objective was not achieved. REP rendezvous was not attempted due to a decision to power down fuel cells.

Secondary objective to demonstrate controlled reentry guidance was not achieved due to incorrect navigation coordinates transmitted to the spacecraft computer from the ground. This caused an 89 mile overshoot of the landing zone. Experiment D-2, Nearby Object Photography was not conducted when REP rendezvous was canceled.

Gemini V

1. Who were the crew members of the Gemini 5 mission?

2. Can you named the backup crew members of this mission?

3. On what date was the Gemini 5 launched?

4. What was the date of the Gemini 5 landing?

5. What was the mission highlights of the Gemini 5?

6. Did any problems occur during this mission?

7. What two primaries were not achieved?

8. What caused an 89 mile overshoot of the landing zone?

9. What was the duration of this mission?

10. How many orbits did this mission have?

Crew:

Frank Borman – Commander
James A. Lovell – Pilot

Backup Crew:

Edward H. White II
Michael Collins

Mission Objective:

Primary objective was to conduct 14-day mission and evaluate effects on crew. Secondary objectives included: Provide target for Gemini VI-A. Station keep with Gemini VI-A, and with second stage of GLV. Conduct 20 experiments. Evaluate lightweight pressure suit. Evaluate spacecraft reentry capability. Conduct systems tests. Spacecraft weight: 3663kg.

Launch:

December 4, 1965; 2:30:03.702 p.m. EST.

Orbit:

Altitude: 327km
Orbits: 206
Duration: 13 days, 18 hours, 35 minutes, 1 second

Landing:

December 18, 1965. Landed at 25 degrees 25.1 min north, 70.6 degrees 7 min west. The miss distance was 11.8km.

Mission highlights:

All primary and secondary objectives were achieved.

Gemini VII

1. Who were the crew members of the Gemini 7?

2. Can you name the backup crew members of this mission?

3. What was the launch date of the Gemini 7?

4. On what date did this mission land?

5. What was the duration of the Gemini 7?

6. How many orbits did this mission have?

7. What were the highlights of this mission?

8. Name two objectives reached by the Gemini 7 mission?

9. How many experiments were to be conducted on this mission?

10. The Gemini 7 missed the target area by how many kilometers?

Crew:

Walter M. Schirra - Commander
Thomas P. Stafford – Pilot

Backup Crew:

Virgil I. Grissom
John W. Young

Mission Objective:

Primary objective was to rendezvous with Gemini-VII. Secondary objectives included: Perform closed-loop rendezvous in fourth orbit. Station keeps with Gemini VII. Evaluate reentry guidance capability. Conduct visibility tests for rendezvous, using Gemini VII as target. Perform 3 experiments. Spacecraft weight 3546kg.

Launch:

December 15, 1965; 8:37:26.471 a.m. Est. Due to a Gemini Agena target vehicle (GATV) propulsion failure on 25 October 1965 the mission was rescheduled. The Agena target vehicle Gemini Agena target vehicle GATV-55002 and TLV 5301 with which the Gemini VI-A was rendezvous and dock, failed to go into orbit. A launch attempt on December 12, 1965 failed because of a minor launch vehicle hardware problem.

Orbit:

Altitude: 311.3km
Orbits: 16
Duration: 1 day, 1hour, 51minutes, 24 seconds

Landing:

December 16, 1965. Landing was at 23 degrees 35min north and 67 degrees 50 min west. Miss distance was 12.9km. The Gemini 6 was recovered by the USS Wasp (crew onboard in 66 minutes).

Mission Highlights:

All primary objectives were achieved. Secondary objective on experiment D-8, radiation in spacecraft because station keeping with Gemini VII interfered with the experiment.

Gemini VI

1. Who were the crew members of the Gemini VI?

2. Can you name the backup crew members of this mission?

3. What was the launch date of the Gemini VI?

4. When was the landing date for this mission?

5. How many orbits did the Gemini VI have?

6. What was the duration of this mission?

7. What were the mission objectives for the Gemini VI?

8. Were all of the primary objectives achieved?

9. What was the mission highlights of the Gemini VI?

10. What was the name of the ship that recovered this mission?

Crew:

Neil A. Armstrong
David R Scott

Backup Crew:

Charles Conrad Jr.
Richard F. Gordon Jr.

Mission Objective:

Primary objective was to rendezvous and dock with Gemini Agena target vehicle (GATV5003) launched on March 16, 1966 from complex 14 (TLV-

5302 and conduct EVA operations. Secondary objective s included: Rendezvous and dock in 4th revolution. Perform docked-vehicle maneuvers. Evaluate systems and conduct 10 experiments. Spacecraft weight: 3788kg. GATV-5003 Weight: 8097.

Launch:

March 16, 1966. 11:41:02.389. there was one day delay in launching the spacecraft due to minor problems with the spacecraft and launch vehicle hardware.

Orbit:

Altitude: 298.7km
Orbits: 7
Duration 0 days, 10 hours, 41 minutes, 26seconds

Landing:

March 17, 1966. Landing was at 25 degrees 13.8min north and 136 degrees 0min east, in the Pacific Ocean. The Gemini 8 was recovered by the USS Mason (crew onboard in 3 hours).

Mission Highlights:

Gemini VIII successfully docked with Gemini Agena target vehicle GATV-6 hours 34 minutes after liftoff. Because of problems with the spacecraft control system, the crew was forced to undock after approximately 30 minutes. The spacecraft-target vehicle combination had begun to encounter increasing yaw and roll rates. The crew regained control of their spacecraft by using the reentry control system, which prompted an early landing in a secondary landing area in the Pacific. No EVA was preformed.
The failure was caused by an electrical short in control system. Docking and rendezvous secondary objectives were not achieved due to the shortened mission.

Gemini VIII

1. Who were the crew members of the Gemini VIII?

2. Can you name the backup crew members of this mission?

3. What was the launch date of the Gemini VIII?

4. When did this mission land?

5. Landing date is associated with what Irish holiday?

6. How many orbits did the Gemini VII?

7. What was the duration of this mission?

8. What was the mission highlights of the Gemini VIII mission?

9. Did any problems occur on this mission?

10. What was the name of the ship that recovered the Gemini VIII?

Crew:

Thomas P. Stafford – Commander
Eugene A. Cernan – Pilot

Backup Crew:

James A. Lovell Jr.
Edwin E. Aldrin

Mission Objective:

Primary objective was to perform rendezvous and docking and conduct EVA. Secondary objectives included: Rendezvous with ATDA (launched 6/1/66 from complex 14) in 3rd revolution. Conduct systems evaluation and equiperiod rendezvous. Execute 7 experiments. Practice Docking, Rendezvous from above and to demonstrate controlled reentry. The original crew of the Gemini IX, Elliott M. See and Charles Bassett were killed in an airplane crash on February 28, 1966. The backup crew was named to the prime crew positions. Spacecraft weight: 3750kg. ATDA weight: 1088kg.

Launch:

June 3, 1966. 8:39:33.335 a.m. EST. GT-9 was postponed when TLV 5303 with Gemini Agena target vehicle GATV-5004 malfunctioned on May 17. In its place, a substitute target was for GT-9A; the Augmented Target Docking Adapter (ATDA) was launched by an Atlas on June 1, 1966 (TLV-5304) from Launch Complex 14: however GT-9A was not launched the same day as planned due to a guidance system computer problem. After a brief hold, the spacecraft was launched on the 3rd day.

Orbit:

Altitude: 311.5km
Orbits: 45
Duration: 3 days, 0 hours, 20minutes, 50 seconds

Landing:

June 6, 1966. Landing was at 27degrees 52min N. and 75degrees 0.4min West. Miss distance: 704 miles. Recovery ship USS Wasp (crew onboard in 52 minutes).

Mission Highlights:

Primary objective of rendezvous and docking was only partially achieved because the shroud on the ATDA failed to jettison. Instead GT-9A performed a number of rendezvous maneuvers, including a simulation of lunar module rendezvous. EVA time 2 hours 7 minutes. During EVA maneuvers, Cernan's visor became fogged, and he was unable to test the Air Force maneuvering unit.

Secondary objective experiment S-10, Agena Micrometerorite Collection experiment was not attempted because EVA did not take place near Gemini Agena target vehicle (GATV).

Gemini IX

1. Who were the crew members of the Gemini-9?

2. Can you name the backup members of this mission?

3. What was the launch date of the Gemini-9?

4. The date that this mission landed was?

5. How many miles off target area did the Gemini-9 land?

6. What was the name of the recovery ship for this mission?

7. How many orbits did the Gemini-9 have?

8. What was the duration of this mission?

9. What was the mission highlights of the Gemini-9?

10. Were all of the objectives reached on this mission?

Crew:

John W. Young
Michael Collins

Backup Crew:

Alan L. Bean
Clifton C. Williams, Jr.

Mission objective:

Primary objective was to rendezvous and dock with Gemini Agena target
vehicle (GATV-5005) launched as TLV-5305 from Complex 14 on July 18,

1966. Secondary objective included: Rendezvous and dock in 4th revolution. Rendezvous with Gemini Agena target vehicle GATV-8 using Agena propulsion system, Conduct EVA, Practice docking, perform 14 experiments, perform system evaluation on bending-mode test, docked maneuvers; static discharge; monitoring; post-docked Agena maneuvers; reentry guidance; park Gemini Agena target vehicle (GATV) in 352km orbit. Spacecraft weight: 3763kg. GATV weight: 8097kg.

Launch:

July 18, 1966. 5:20:26.648 p.m. EST.

Orbit:

Altitude: 753.3km
Orbits: 43
Duration: 2 days, 22 hours, 46minutes. 39 seconds

Landing:

July 21, 1966. 4:07 p.m. Landing was at 26 degrees 44.7 min north and 71 degrees 57 min west. Miss distance was 6.2km.

Mission highlights:

1hour, 29 minutes EVA. All primary objective and most secondary objectives were met the practice docking secondary objective and some experiments were canceled due to insufficient fuel reserves.

Gemini X

1. Who were the crew members of the Gemini-10?

2. Can you name the backup crew members of this mission?

3. When was the Gemini-10 launched?

4. What date did this mission landed?

5. How many orbits did the Gemini-10 have?

6. What was the duration of this mission?

7. Were all of the primary objectives reached on the Gemini-10 mission?

8. How many experiments were to be performed on this mission?

9. What were the mission highlights for the Gemini-10 mission?

10. What caused the secondary objectives to be cancelled on the mission?

Crew:

     Charles Conrad, Jr.
     Richard F. Gordon, Jr.

Backup Crew:

     Neil A Armstrong
     William A. Anders

Mission Objective:

Primary objective was to rendezvous and dock with Gemini Agena target vehicle (GATV-5006) which was launched September 12, 1966 from Launch Complex 14 as TLV-5306 in 1st revolution. Secondary objectives included. Practice docking, and perform EVA. Conduct 11 experiments, Maneuver while docked (high apogee excursion), Conduct tethered vehicle test, Demonstrate reentry and Park GATV-10 in 352.4km orbit. Spacecraft weight: 3798kg. GATV weight: 8097kg.

1

Launch:

September 12, 1966. 9:42:26.546 a.m. EST. The launch was postponed twice; On September 9 due to a small leak in the first stage oxidizer tank of the GLV; and on the 10th due to a suspected malfunction of the autopilot on the GLV. On the day of the launch there was a 16 minute hold due to a suspected leak around the command pilot's hatch.

Orbit

Altitude: 1368.9km
Orbits: 44
Duration: 2 days 23 hours 17 minutes 8 seconds

Landing:

September 15, 1966. Landing was at 24 degrees 15.4 min north and 70 degrees 0.0 min west. Miss distance was 4.9km. Recovery ship USS Guam (crew onboard in 24 minutes).

Mission highlights:

All primary objectives and most secondary objectives were achieved. Experiment D-16, Power Tool Evaluation was canceled when the EVA was terminated early. During EVA, astronaut Gordon tethered the two spacecraft together with a 30-meter line. Automatic reentry was successful.

Gemini XI

1. Who were the crew members of the Gemini 11 mission?

2. Can you name the backup crew member for this mission?

3. On what date was the Gemini 11 launched?

4. What was the landing date of this mission?

5. How many orbits did this mission have?

6. What was the duration of the Gemini 11 mission?

7. Was automatic reentry successful?

8. What was the mission highlights for the gemini11?

9. Did this mission reach all of its primary objectives?

10. What happened to the Power Tool Evaluation on this mission?

Crew:

James A Lovell, Jr.: Commander
Edwin E. Aldrin: Pilot

Backup Crew:

L. Gordon Cooper, Jr.
Eugene A Cernan

Mission objective:

Primary objective was rendezvous and docking and to evaluate EVA. Secondary objective included: Tethered vehicle operation, perform 14 experiments, rendezvous and dock in 3rd revolution, demonstrate automatic reentry, perform docked maneuvers, practice docking, conduct system test and to park Gemini Agena target vehicle GATV-12 in 555.6km orbit.

Launch:

November 11, 1966. 3:46:33.419 p.m. EST

Orbit:

Altitude: 301.3km
Orbits: 59
Duration: 3 days, 22 hours, 34 minutes, 31 seconds

Landing:

Was on November 15, 1966; landed at 24degrees 35min north 69degrees 57min west. Miss distance was 4.8km.

Mission Highlights:

EVA time 5 hours, 30 minutes. All primary objectives and most secondary objectives were met. Docked maneuvers were canceled due to a propulsion anomaly during Gemini Agena target vehicle (GATV) insertion. The GATV was not placed in a 555.6km orbit because its altitude control gas was depleted by earlier maneuvers.

Gemini XII

1. Who were the crew members of the Gemini 12?

2. Can you name the backup members of this mission?

3. On what date was the Gemini 12 launched?

4. What was the landing date for this mission?

5. How many orbits did the Gemini 12 have?

6. The landing missed the target area by how much?

7. What was the duration of the Gemini 12 mission?

8. The mission high lights for this mission were?

9. What caused the docking maneuvers to cancel out on the Gemini 12?

10. How many experiments were to be performed on this mission?

Crew:

> Vigil I. Grissom
> Edward H. White II
> Roger B. Chaffee

Backup Crew:

> Walter M. Schirra, Jr.
> Donn F. Eisele
> Walter Cunningham

Mission Objective:

> January 27, 1967. Tragedy struck on the launch pad during a preflight test
> for Apollo 204 (AS-204), which was scheduled to be the first Apollo
> manned mission, and would have been launched on February 21, 1967.
> Astronauts Virgil Grissom, Edward White, and Roger Chaffee lost their
> lives when a fire swept through the Command Module (CM).
>
> The exhaustive investigation of the fire and extensive reworking of the CMs
> postponed any manned launch until NASA officials cleared the CM for
> manned flight. Saturn 1B schedules were suspended for nearly a year, and
> the launch vehicle that finally bore the designation AS-204 carried a Lunar
> Module (LM) as the payload, not the Apollo CM. The missions of AS-201
> and AS-202 with Apollo spacecraft aboard had been unofficially known as

Apollo 1 and Apollo 2 missions (AS-203 carried only the aerodynamic nose cone). In the spring of 1967, NASA's Associate Administrator for Manned Space Flight, Dr. George E. Muller, announced that the mission originally scheduled for Grissom, White and Chaffee would be known as Apollo 1, and said that the first Saturn V launch, scheduled for November 1967, would be known as Apollo 4. The eventual launch of AS-204 became known as the Apollo 5 mission (no missions or flights were ever designated Apollo 2 and 3).

The second launch of a Saturn V took place on schedule in the early morning of April 4, 1968. Known as AS-502, or Apollo 6, the flight was a success, though two first stage engines shut down prematurely, and the third stage engine failed to re-ignite after reaching orbit.

Apollo 1

1. Who were the crew members of the Apollo 1?

2. Can you name the backup crew members of this mission?

3. Was there a launch or landing for the Apollo 1?

4. What happened to this mission? (explain in detail)

5. Was there ever a mission or flight named Apollo 2or 3?

Crew:

Walter M. Schirra, Jr.: Commander
Donn F. Eisele: CSM Pilot
R. Walter Cunningham: Lunar Module Pilot

Backup Crew

Thomas Stafford: Commander
John Young: CSM Pilot
Eugene Cernan: Lunar Module Pilot

Mission objectives:

The primary objective for the Apollo 7 engineering test flight, were simple: "Demonstrate CSM/crew performance; demonstrate crew/space vehicle/mission support facilities performance during a manned CSM mission; demonstrate CSM rendezvous capability."

Launch:

October 11, 1968. 11:02:45 am EST. October 11 at Cape Kennedy was hot but the heat was tempered by a pleasant breeze when Apollo 7 lifted off in a two-tongued blaze of orange-colored flame. The Saturn IB, in its first trial with men aboard, provided a perfect launch and its first stage dropped off 2 minutes 25 seconds later. The S-IVB second stage took over, giving astronauts their first ride atop a load of liquid hydrogen, and at 5 minutes 54 seconds into the mission, Walter Schirra, the commander, reported, "She is riding like a dream." About five minutes later an elliptical orbit had been achieved, 140 by 183 miles above the earth. Launch Weight: xxx, xxx lbs.

Orbit:

Altitude: 140 x 183 miles
Orbits: 163
Duration: 10 days, 20 hours.

Landing:

The CSM's service propulsion system, which had to fire the CSM into and out of moon orbit, worked perfectly during eight burns lasting from half a second to 67.6 seconds. Apollo's flotation bags had their first try-out when the spacecraft, a "lousy boat," splashed down in the Atlantic southeast of Bermuda, less than two kilometers from the planed impact point. Landing location was 27deg 32min north and 64deg 04min west. The module turned upside down; when inflated, the brightly colored bags flipped it aright. The tired, but happy, voyagers were picked up by helicopter and deposited on the deck of the U.S.S. Essex by 08:20 am EDT. The spacecraft was aboard the ship at 09:03 am.

Mission Highlights:

Once Apollo 7 cleared the pad, a three-shift mission control team-led by flight directors Glynn Lunney, Eugene Kranz, and Gerald D. Griffin in Houston took over. Schirra, Eisele, and Cunningham inside the command module had listened to the sound of propellants rushing into the firing chamber had noticed the vehicle swaying slightly, and had left the vibrations at ignition. Ten and a half minutes after launch, with little bumpiness and low g loads during acceleration, Apollo 7 reached the first stage of its journey, an orbital path 227 by 285 kilometers above the earth.

The S-IVB stayed with the CSM for about one and one-half orbits, and then separated. Schirra fired the CSM's small rockets to pull 50 feet ahead of the S-IVB, and then turned the spacecraft around to simulate docking, as would be necessary to extract an LM for a moon landing. The next day when the CSM and the S-IVB, were about 80 miles apart, Schirra and his mates sought out the lifeless, tumbling 59-foot craft in a rendezvous simulation and approached within 70 feet.

Walter Cunningham reported the spacecraft-lunar module adapter panels had not fully deployed, which naturally reminded Stafford, on the capsule communicator (CapCom) console, of the "angry alligator" target vehicle he had encountered on his Gemini IX mission. This mishap would have been embarrassing on a mission that carried a lunar module. But the panels would be jettisoned explosively on future flights.

After this problem, service module engine performance was a joy. This was one area where the crew could not switch to a redundant or backup system; at crucial times during a lunar voyage, the engine simply had to work or they would not get back home. On Apollo 7, there were eight nearly perfect firings out of eight attempts. On the first, the crew had a real surprise. In contrast to the smooth liftoff of the Saturn, the blast from the service module engine jolted the astronauts, causing Schirra to yell "Yabadabadoo" like Fred Flintstone in the contemporary video cartoon. Later Eisele said, "We didn't quite know what to expect, but we got more than we expected." He added more graphically that it was a real boot in the rear that just plastered them into their seats. But the engine did what it was supposed to do each time it fired.

The Apollo vehicle and the CSM performed superbly. Durability was shown for 10.8 days, longer than a journey to the moon and back. With few exceptions, the other systems in the spacecraft operated as they should. Occasionally, one of the three fuel cells supplying electricity to the craft developed some unwanted high temperatures, but load-sharing hookups among the cells prevented any power shortage. The crew complained about noisy fans in the environmental circuits and turned one of them off. That did not help much, so the men switched off the other. The cabin stayed comfortable, although the coolant lines sweated and water collected in little puddles on the deck, which the crew expected after the Kerwin team's test in the altitude chamber. Schirra's crew vacuumed the excess water out into space with the urine dump hose. A momentary shudder went through Mission Control when both AC buses dropped out of the spacecraft's electrical system, coincident with automatic cycles of the cryogenic oxygen tank fans and heaters; but manual resetting of the AC bus breakers restored normal service.

Three of the five spacecraft windows fogged because of improperly cured sealant compound (a condition that could not be fixed until Apollo 9). Visibility from the spacecraft windows ranged from poor to good, during the mission. Shortly after the launch escape tower jettisoned, two of the windows had soot deposits and two others had water condensation. Two days later, however, Cunningham reported that most of the windows were in fairly good shape, although moisture was collecting between the inner panes of one window. On the seventh day, Schirra described essentially the same conditions.

Even with these impediments, the windows were adequate. Those used for observations during rendezvous and station keeping with the S-IVB remained almost clear. Navigational sighting with a telescope and a sextant on any of the preselected "Apollo" stars was difficult if done too soon after a waste-water dump. Sometime they had to wait several minutes for the frozen particles to disperse. Eisele reported that unless he could see 40 or 50 stars at a time he found it hard to decide what part of the sky he was looking toward. On the whole, however, the windows were satisfactory for general and landmark observations and for out-the-window photography.

Most components supported the operations and well-being of the spacecraft and crew as planned, in spite of minor irritations like smudging windows and puddling water. For example, the waste management system for collecting solid body wastes was adequate, though annoying. The defecation bags, containing a germicide to prevent bacteria and gas formation, were easily sealed and stored in empty food containers in the equipment bay. But the bags were certainly not convenient and there were usually unpleasant odors. Each time they were used, it took the crew member from 45 to 60 minutes, causing him to postpone it as long as possible, waiting for a time when there was no work to do. The crew had a total of only 12 defecation over a period of nearly 11 days. Urination was much easier, as the crew did not have to remove clothing. There was a collection service for both the pressure suits and the in-flight coveralls. Both devices could be attached to the urine dump hose and emptied into space. They had half expected the hose valve to freeze up in vacuum, but it never did.

Chargers for the batteries needed for reentry (after fuel cells departed with the SM) returned 50 to 75 percent less energy than expected. Most serious was the overheating of fuel cells, which might have failed when the spacecraft was too far from earth to return on batteries, even if fully charged. But each of these anomalies was satisfactorily checked out before Apollo 8 flew.

Some of the crew's grumpiness during the mission could be attributed to physical discomfort. About 15 hours into the flight, Schirra developed a bad cold, and Cunningham and Eisele soon followed suit. A cold is uncomfortable enough on the ground; in weightless space it presents a different problem. Mucus accumulates, filling the nasal passages, and does not drain from the head. The only relief is to blow hard, which is painful to the eardrums. So the crewmen of Apollo 7 traveled through space suffering from stopped up ears and noses. They took aspirin and decongestant tablets and discussed their symptoms with the doctors.

Several days before the mission ended, they began to worry about wearing their suit helmets during reentry, which would prevent them from blowing their noses. The buildup of pressure might burst their eardrums. Slayton, in mission control, tried to persuade them to wear the helmets, anyway, but Schirra was adamant. They each took a decongestant pill about an hour before reentry and made it through the acceleration zone without any problems with their ears.

Apollo 7 accomplished what it set out to do qualifying the command and service module and clearing the way for the proposed lunar-orbit mission to follow. And its activities were of national interest. A special edition of

NASA's news clipping collection called "Current News" included front page stories from 32 major newspapers scattered over the length and breadth of the nation. Although the post-mission celebrations may not have rivaled those for the first orbital flight of an American, John Glenn in 1962, enthusiasm was high and this fervor would build to even greater heights each time the lunar landing goal drew one step closer. In retrospect it seems inconceivable, but serious debate ensued in NASA councils on whether television should be broadcast from Apollo missions, and the decision to carry the little 4 ½ pound camera was not made until just before this October flight. Although these early pictures were crude, I think it was informative for the public to see astronauts floating weightlessly in their roomy spacecraft, snatching floating objects, and eating the first hot food consumed in space. Like the television pictures, the food improved in later missions.

Apollo 7's achievement led to a rapid review of Apollo 8's options. The Apollo 7 astronauts went through six days of debriefing for the benefit of Apollo 8, and on October 28 the Manned Space Flight Management Council chaired by Mueller met at MSC, investigating every phase of the forthcoming mission. Next day came a lengthy systems review of Apollo 8's Spacecraft 103. Paine made the go/no- goes review of lunar orbit on November 11 at NASA Headquarters in Washington. By this time nearly all the skeptics had become converts.

Apollo VII

1. Who were the crew members of the Apollo 7 mission?

2. Can you name the backup crew members of this mission?

3. On what date was the Apollo 7 launched?

4. When did this mission land?

5. What was the duration of the Apollo 7 mission?

6. How many orbits did this mission have?

7. What were the mission objectives on the Apollo 7 mission?

8. Did any problems occur on this mission? If so, explain in detail.

9. What was the mission highlights of the Apollo 7 mission?

10. What was the name of the recovery ship on this mission?

Crew:

Frank Borman: Commander
James A. Lovell, Jr.
William A. Anders

Mission Objective:

Demonstrate crew/space vehicle/mission support facilities during manned
Saturn V/CSM mission. Demonstrate translunar injection, CSM navigation,
communications, and midcourse corrections. Assess CSM consumables and
passive thermal control. Demonstrate communications and tracking at lunar
distances. Return high-resolution photographs of proposed Apollo landing
sites and locations of scientific interest. All mission objectives were
achieved.

Launch:

December 21, 1968, 07:51:00 a.m. EST. Kennedy Space Center Launch Complex 39-A.

Orbit:

Altitude: 190km x 180km
Orbit: 10
Duration: 6 days, 3 hours, 0 minutes, 42 seconds

Landing:

December 27, 1968; 10:52 am EST; Landing point 8 degrees 7.5 min north and 165 degrees 1.2 min west. Miss distance was 2.5km; Splashdown time, December 27, 1968 at 10:52 a.m. EST; MET: 147:00:42. Crew was on board U.S.S Yorktown at 12:20 p.m. EST; Spacecraft was aboard ship at 01:20 p.m.

Mission Highlights:

Apogee was 190 kilometers. Perigee was 180 kilometers. Translunar injection at 02:56:05.5 Met; lunar orbit 312km by 111km; transearth injection, 89:19:17 MET.

In lunar was orbit 20 hours, with 10 orbits. This was the first manned lunar orbital mission. Support facilities were tested. Photographs were taken of earth and moon, and a live TV broadcasts.

Apollo VIII

1. Who were the crew members on the Apollo 8 mission?

2. Were there any backup crew members for this mission?

3. What was the launch date for the Apollo 8 mission?

4. The landing date for this mission was?

5. How many orbits did the Apollo 8 mission have?

6. The duration of this mission was?

7. What were the mission objectives of the Apollo 8 mission?

8. The mission highlights for this mission were?

9. What was the name of the recovery ship for the Apollo 8 mission?

10. Were all of the mission objectives achieved on this mission?

Crew:

James A. McDivitt
David R. Scott
Russell L. Schweickart

Mission objective:

Demonstrate crew/space vehicle/mission support facilities during manned
Saturn V/CSM/LM mission (Achieved). Demonstrate LM/crew performance
(Achieved). Demonstrate selected lunar orbit rendezvous and docking. All

1

achieved except EVA (because of schweickart's illness, most EVA's were canceled). Assess CSM/LM consumables used.

Launch:

March 03, 1969; 11:00:00 am EST. Launch Complex 39-A Kennedy Space Center. No delays.

Orbit:

Altitude: 192km x 190km
Orbits: 152
Duration: 10 days, 01 hours, 01 minute

Landing:

March 13, 1969 at 12:01 p.m. EST; the landing point was 23degrees 12.5 min. north and 67 degrees 56min. west (Atlantic Ocean). Miss distance 4.8 kilometers. Crew was on board the U.S.S Guadalcanal at 12:45 pm EST; spacecraft aboard the ship at 02:13 pm.

Mission Highlights:

Apogee was 192 km. Perigee was 190 km. The first manned Apollo docking 03:01:59 MET; first docked SPS burn, 05:59:01 MET; Apollo EVA, 72:53:00 MET. First manned Apollo undocking, 92:39:36 MET; first manned LM to CSM docking, 99:02:26 MET.

It was the first manned flight of all lunar hardware in earth orbit. Schweickart performed 37 minutes EVA. Human reactions to space and weightlessness tested in 152 orbits. The first manned flight of lunar module.

Apollo IX

1. Who were the crew members of the Apollo-9 mission?

2. What was the launch date of this mission?

3. The landing date of the Apollo- 9 mission was?

4. How many orbits did this mission have?

5. What was the duration of the Apollo-9 mission?

6. The mission objectives for this mission were?

7. Was the entire objective reached on the Apollo -9 mission?

8. What was the mission highlights of this mission?

9. Why were most of the EVA's canceled on the Apollo-9 mission?

10. Can you name the recovery ship for this mission?

Crew:

      Eugene A. Cernan
      John W. Young
      Thomas P. Stafford

Mission Objective:

      Demonstrate performance of LM and CSM in lunar gravitation field.
      Evaluate CSM and LM docked and undocked lunar navigation. All mission
      objectives were achieved.

Launch:

      On May 18, 1969; at12:49:00 a.m. EDT Kennedy Space Center FL. No
      delays.

Orbit:

Altitude: 190km x 184km
Orbits: 31
Duration: 08 days, 0 hours, 03minutes, 23 seconds

Landing:

May 26, 1969. 12:52 am EDT. Landing point was 15 degrees 2min. south by 164 degrees 39min. west. Miss distance not available. Crew was on board U.S.S Princeton at 01:31 p.m. EDT; the spacecraft was aboard ship at 02:28 p.m.

Mission Highlights:

Apogee was 190 kilometers; Perigee was kilometers; translunar injection, 02:39:21 MET; maximum distance from earth, 399,194km; first CSM-LM docking in translunar trajectory, 03:17:37 MET; lunar orbit insertion, 75:55:54 MET; first LM undocking in lunar orbit, 98:11:57 MET; first LM staging in lunar orbit, 102:45:17 MET; first manned LM-CSM docking in lunar orbit, 106:22:02 MET; transearth injection 137:36:29 MET.

This was dress rehearsal for moon landing. Was the first manned CSM/LM operations in cislunar and lunar environment; simulation of first lunar landing profile. Lunar orbit was 61.6 hours, with 31 orbits. LM was taken to within 15,243m (50,000 ft) of lunar surface. This was the first live color TV from space. LM was ascent stage jettisoned in orbit.

Apollo X

1. Who were the crew members of the Apollo-10 mission?

2. What was the launch date for this mission?

3. When did the Apollo-10 mission land?

4. How many orbits did this mission have?

5. What was the duration of the Apollo-10 mission?

6. The mission objective for this mission was?

7. What was the mission highlights for the Apollo-10?

8. Why was this mission necessary?

9. What was the name of the recovery ship for the Apollo-10?

10. At what time did the spacecraft come aboard the ship?

Crew:

Neil A. Armstrong: Commander
Edwin E. Aldrin, Jr.: Lunar Module Pilot
Michael Collins: Command Module Pilot

The National Aeronautics and Space Administration (NASA) have named these three astronauts as the prime crew of the Apollo 11 lunar landing mission.

Backup Crew:

James Lovell: Backup Commander
Fred Haise: Backup Lunar Module Pilot
William A. Anders: Backup Command Module Pilot

Mission Objective:

Perform manned lunar landing and return mission safely. (Was achieved)

Launch:

July 16, 1969. 09:32:00 am EDT. Launch Complex 39-A Kennedy Space Center, FL. No launch delays.

The splashdown May 26, 1969, of the Apollo 10 cleared the way for the first formal attempt at a manned lunar landing. Six days before, the Apollo 11 launch vehicle and spacecraft half crawled from the VAB and trundled at 0.9 mph to Pad 39-A. A successful countdown test ending on July 3rd showed the readiness of machines, systems, and people. The next launch window (established by lighting conditions at the landing site on Mare Tranquillitatis) opened at 9:32 am EDT on July 16, 1969. The crew for Apollo 11, all of whom had already flown in space during Gemini, had been intensively training as a team for many months. The following mission account makes use of crew member's own words, from books written by two of them, supplemented by space-to-ground and press-conference transcripts.

ALDRIN: At breakfast early on the morning of the launch. Dr. Thomas Paine, the Administrator of NASA, told us "that concern for our own safety must govern all our actions, and if anything looked wrong we were to abort the mission". He then made a most surprising and unprecedented statement: if we were forced to abort, we would be immediately recycled and assigned to the next landing attempt. What he said and how he said it was very reassuring.

We were up early, ate, and began to suit up, a rather laborious and detailed procedure involving many people, which we would repeat once again, alone, before entering the LM for our lunar landing.

While Mike and Neil were going through the complicated business of being strapped in and connected to the spacecraft's life-support system, I waited near the elevator on the floor below. I waited alone for fifteen minutes in a sort of serene limbo. As far as I could see there were people and cars lining the beaches and highways. The surf was just beginning to rise out of an azure-blue ocean. I could see the massiveness of the Saturn V rocket below and the magnificent precision of Apollo above. I savored the wait and marked the minutes in my mind as something I would always want to remember.

COLLINS: I am everlastingly thankful that I have flown before, and that this period of waiting atop a rocket is nothing new. I am just as tense this time, but tenseness comes mostly from an appreciation of the enormity of our undertaking rather than from the unfamiliarity of the situation. I am far from certain that we will be able to fly the mission as planned. I think we will escape with our skins, or at least I will escape with mine, but I wouldn't give better than even odds on a successful landing and return. There are just too many things that can go wrong. Fred Haise [the backup astronaut who had checked command-module switch positions] has run through a checklist 417 steps long. And I have merely a half dozen minor chores to take care of nickel and dime stuff. In between switch throws I have plenty of time to think, if not daydream. Here I am, a white male, age thirty-eight, height 5 feet 11 inches, weight 165 pounds, salary $17,000 per annum, resident of a Texas suburb, with black spot on my roses, state of mind unsettled, about to be shot off to the moon. Yes, to the moon.

At the moment, the most important control is over on Neil's side, just outboard of his left knee. It is the abort handle, and now it has power to it, so if Neil rotates it 30degrees counterclockwise, three solid rockets above us will fire and yank the CM free of the service module and everything below it. It is only to be used in extremes. A large bulky pocket has been added to Neil's left suit leg, and it looks as though if he moves his leg slightly, it's going to snag on the abort handle. I quickly point this out to Neil, and he grabs the pocket and pulls it as far over to the inside of his thigh as he can, but it still doesn't look secure to either one of us. Jesus, I can see the headlines now: "MOONSHOT FALLS INTO OCEAN." Mistaken by crew, program officials intimate. Last transmission from Armstrong prior to leaving the pad reportedly was "Oops."

ARMSTRONG: The flight started promptly, and I think that was characteristic of all events of the flight. The Saturn gave us one magnificent ride, both earth orbit and on a trajectory to the moon. Our memory of that differs little from the reports you have heard from the previous Saturn V flights.

ALDRIN: For the thousands of people watching along the beaches of Florida and the millions who watched on television, our lift-off was ear shattering. For us there was a slight increase in the amount of background noise, not at all unlike the sort one notices taking off in a commercial airliner, and in less than a minute we were traveling ahead of the speed of sound.

COLLINS: This beast is best felt. Shake, rattle, and roll, we are thrown left and right against our straps in spasmodic little jerks. It is steering like crazy, like a nervous lady driving a wide car down a narrow alley, and I just hope it knows where it's going, because for the first ten seconds we are perilously close to that umbilical tower.

ALDRIN: A busy eleven minutes later we were in earth orbit. The earth didn't look much different from the way it had during my first flight, and yet I kept looking at it. From space it has an almost benign quality. Intellectually one could realize there were wars underway, but emotionally it was impossible to understand such things. The thought reoccurred that wars are generally fought for territory or are disputes over borders; from space the arbitrary borders established on earth cannot be seen. After one and a half orbits a preprogrammed sequence fired the Saturn to send us out of earth orbit and on our way to the moon.

Orbit:

Altitude: 186km x 183km
Duration: 08 days, 03 hours, 18min, 35 seconds
Lunar Location: Sea of Tranquility
Lunar Coords: .71 degrees north, 23.63 degrees east

Landing:

July 24, 1969. 12:50 p.m. EDT. Splashdown area 13 degrees 19 min north and 169 degrees 9 min west; Splashdown at 195:18:35 MET. Crew was on board U.S.S Hornet at 01:53 p.m. EDT; spacecraft aboard ship at 03:50 p.m.

Mission Highlights:

Apogee, 186km; Perigee 183km; translunar injection 02:44:26 MET; maximum distance from earth 389,645km; lunar orbit insertion, 75:50:00 MET; lunar landing, 102:45:39 MET (20 July at 04:17 p.m. EDT). First step on moon 10:56:15 p.m. EDT; end of EVA, 111:39:13 MET (01:09 a.m. EDT); liftoff from moon, 124:22:00.8 MET (1:54 p.m. EDT); LM-CSM docking, 128:03:00 MET; transearth injection, 135:23:52.3 MET;

The first manned lunar landing mission and lunar surface EVA. "HOUSTON TRANQUILITY BASE HERE. THE EAGLE HAS LANDED." It was July 20, at the Sea of Tranquility.

1 EVA of 02 hours, 31minutes. Flag and instruments deployed; unveiled plaque on the LM descent stage with inscription: "Here Men from Planet Earth First Set Foot upon the Moon. July 1969 A.D. We Came IN Peace For All Mankind." Lunar surface stay time 21.6 hours; 59.5 hours in lunar orbit, with 30 orbits. LM ascent stage left in lunar orbit. 20 kg (44lbs) of material gathered.

ARMSTRONG: HEY Houston, Apollo 11. This Saturn gave us a magnificent ride. We have no complaints with any of the three stages on that ride. It was beautiful.

COLLINS: We started the burn at 100 miles altitude, and had reached only 180 at cutoff, but we are climbing like a dingbat. In nine hours, when we are scheduled to make our first midcourse correction, we will be 57,000 miles out. At the instant of shutdown, Buzz recorded our velocity as 35,579 feet per second, more than enough to escape from the earth gravitational field. As we proceed outbound, this number will get smaller and smaller until the tug of the moon's gravity exceeds that of the earths and then we will start speeding up again. It's hard to believe that we are on our way to the moon, at 1200 miles altitude now, less than three hours after liftoff, and I'll bet the launch-day crowd down at the cape is still bumper to bumper, straggling back to the motels and bars.

ALDRIN: Mike's next major task, with Neil and me assisting, was to separate our command module Columbia from the Saturn third stage, turn around and connect with the lunar module Eagle, which was stored in the third stage. Eagle, by now, was exposed; its four enclosing panels had automatically come off and were drifting away. This of course was a critical maneuver in the flight plan. If the separation and docking did not work, we would return to Earth. There was also the possibility of an in-space collision and the subsequent decompression of out cabin, so we were still in our spacesuits as Mike separated us from the Saturn third stage. Critical as the maneuver is, I felt no apprehension about it, and if there was the slightest inkling of concern it disappeared quickly as the entire separation and docking proceeded perfectly to completion. The nose of Columbia was now connected to the top of the Eagle and heading for the moon as we watched slowly away from us. Fourteen hours after liftoff, at 10:30 PM by Houston time, the three astronauts fasten covers over the windows of the slowly rotating command module and go to sleep. Days 2 and 3 are devoted to housekeeping chores, a small midcourse velocity correction, and TV transmissions back to earth. In one news digest form Huston, the astronauts are amused to hear that Pravda

ALDRIN: In our preliminary flight plan I wasn't scheduled to go to the LM until the next day in lunar orbit. But I had lobbied successfully to go earlier. My strongest argument was that I'd have ample time to make sure that the frail LM and its equipment had suffered no damage during the launch and long trip. By that time neither Neil nor I had been in the LM for about two weeks.

The Most Awesome Sphere:

COLLINS: Day 4 has a decidedly different feel to it. Instead of nine hours' conserve our energy on the way to the moon, the pressure is overtaking us and we are about to lay our little pink bodies on the line. Our first shock comes as we stop our spinning motion and swing ourselves around so as to bring the moon into view. We have not been able to see the moon for nearly a day now, and the change is electrifying. The moon I have known all my life, that two- dimensional small yellow disk in the sky, has gone away somewhere, to be replaced by the most awesome sphere I have ever seen. To begin with it is huge, completely filling our window. Second, it is three-dimensional. The belly of it bulges out toward us in such a pronounced fashion that I almost feel I can reach out and touch it. To add to the dramatic effect, we can see the stars again. We are in the shadow of the moon now, and the elusive stars have reappeared.

As we ease around on the left side of the moon, I marvel again at the precision of our path. We have missed hitting the moon by a paltry 300 and don't forget that the moon is a moving target and that we are racing through the sky just ahead of its leading edge. When we launched the other day the moon was nowhere near where it is now; it was some 40 degrees of arc, or nearly 200,000 miles, behind where it is now, and yet those big computers in the basement in Houston didn't even whimper but belched out super-accurate predictions.

As we pass behind the moon, we have just over eight minutes to go before the burn. We are super-careful now, checking and rechecking each step several times. When the moment finally arrives, the big engine instantly springs into action and reassuringly plasters us back in our seats. The acceleration is only a fraction of one G but it feels good nonetheless. For six minutes we sit there peering intent as hawks at our instrument panel, being done to us. When the engine shuts down, we discuss the matter with our instrument panel, scanning the important dials and gauges, making sure that the proper thing is being done to us. When the engine shuts down, we discuss the matter with our computer and I read out the results: "Minus one, plus one, plus one." The accuracy of the overall system is phenomenal: out of a total of nearly three thousand feet per second, we have velocity errors in our body axis coordinate system of only a tenth of one foot per second in each of the three directions. That is one accurate burn, and even Neil acknowledges the facts.

ALDRIN: The second burn to place us in closer circular orbit of the moon, the orbit from which Neil and I would separate from the Columbia and continue on to the moon, was critically important. It had to be made in exactly the right place and for exactly the correct length of time. If we over burned for as little as two seconds we'd be on an impact course for the other side of the moon. Through a complicated and detailed system of checks and balances, both in Houston and in lunar orbit, plus star checks and detailed platform alignments, two hours after our first lunar orbit we made our second burn, in an atmosphere of nervous and intense concentration. It, too, worked perfectly. "

Asleep in Lunar Orbit:

We began preparing the LM. It was scheduled to take three hours, but because I had already started the checkout, we were completed a half hour ahead of scheduled. Reluctantly we returned to the Columbia as planned. Our fourth night we were to sleep in lunar orbit. Although it was not in the flight plan, before covering the windows and dousing the lights, Neil and I carefully prepared all the equipment and clothing we would need in the morning, and mentally ran through the many procedures we would follow.

COLLINS:"Apollo 11, Apollo 11, good morning from the Black Team." Could they be talking to me? It takes me twenty seconds to fumble for the microphone button and answer groggily, I guess I have only been asleep five hours or so; I had a tough time getting to sleep, and now I'm having trouble waking up. Neil, Buzz, and I all putter about fixing breakfast and getting various items ready for transfer into the LM. [Later] I stuff Neil and Buzz into the LM along with an armload of equipment. Now I have to do the tunnel bit again, closing hatches, installing drogue and probe, and disconnecting the electrical umbilical. I am on the radio constantly now, running through an elaborate series of joint checks with Eagle. I check progress with Buzz: "I have five minutes and fifteen seconds since we started. Attitude is holding well." "Roger, Mike, just hold it a little bit longer." "No sweat, I can hold it all day. Take your sweet time. How's the czar over there? He's so quiet." Neil chimes in, "Just hanging on and punching." Punching those computer buttons, I guess he means "All I can say is beware the revolution," and then, getting no answer, I formally bid them goodbye. "You cats take it easy on the lunar surface…" "O.K., Mike," Buzz answers cheerily, and I throw the switch which releases them. With my nose against the window and the movie camera churning away, I watch them go. When they are safely clear of me, I inform Neil, and he begins a slow pirouette in place, allowing me a look at his outlandish machine and its four extended legs. "The Eagle has wings" Neil exults. It doesn't look like any eagle I have ever seen. It is the weirdest looking contraption ever to invade the sky, floating there with its legs awkwardly jutting out above a body which has neither symmetry nor grace. I make sure all four landing gears are down and locked, report that fact, and then lie a little, "I think you've got a fine looking flying machine there. Eagle, despite the fact you're upside down." "Somebody's upside down." Neil retorts. "O.K., Eagle. One minute… you guys take care." Neil answers, "See you later." I hope so. When the minute is up, I fire my thrusters precisely as planned and we begin to separate, checking distances and velocities as we go. This burn is a very small one, just to give Eagle some breathing room. From now on it's up to them, and they will make two separate burns in reaching the lunar surface. The first one will serve to drop Eagle's perilune to fifty thousand feet. Then, when they reach this spot over the eastern edge of the Sea of Tranquility, Eagle's decent engine will be fired up for the second and last time, and Eagle will lazily arc over into a 12 minute computer controlled descent to some point at which Neil will take over for a manual landing.

ALDRIN: We were still 60 miles above the surface when we began our first burn. Neil and I were harnessed into the LM in a standing position. [Later] at precisely the right moment the engine ignited to begin the 12 minute descent. Strapped in by the system of belts and cables not unlike shock absorbers, neither of us felt the initial motion. We looked quickly at the computer to make sure we were actually functioning as planned. After 26 seconds the engine went to full throttle and the motion became noticeable. Neil watched his instruments while I looked at our primary computer and compared it with our second computer, which was part of our abort guidance system.

I then began a computer read out sequence to Neil which was also being transmitted to Houston. I had helped develop it. It sounded as though I was chattering like a magpie. It also sounded as though I was doing all the work. During training we had discussed the possibility of making the communication only between Neil and me, but Mission Control liked the idea of hearing our communications with each other. Neil had referred to it once as "that damned open mike of yours," and I tried to make as little an issue of it as possible.

A Yellow Caution Light:

At six thousand feet above the lunar surface a yellow caution light came on and we encounter one of the few potentially serious problems in the entire flight, a problem which might have caused us to abort, had it not been for a man on the ground who really knew his job.

COLLINS: At five minutes into the burn, when I am directly overhead, Eagle voices its first concern. "Program Alarm," barks Neil, "It's a 1202." What the hell is that? I don't have the alarm numbers memorized for my own computer, much less for the LM's. I jerk out my own checklist and start thumbing through it, but before I can find 1202, Houston says, "Roger, we're GO on the alarm." No problem, in other words. My checklist says 1202 is an "executive overflow," meaning simply that the computer has been called upon to do too many things at once and is forced to postpone some of them. A little farther along, at just three thousand feet above the surface, the computer flashes 1201, another overflow condition, and again the ground is super quick to respond with reassurances.

ALDRIN: Back in Houston, not to mention on board the Eagle, hearts shot up into throats while we waited to learn what would happen. We had received two of the caution lights when Steve Bales the flight controller responsible for LM computer activity, told us to proceed, through Charlie Duke, the capsule communicator. We received three or four more warnings but kept on going. When Mike, Neil, and I were presented with Medals of Freedom by President Nixon, Steve also received one. He certainly deserved it, because without him we might not have landed.

ARMSTRONG: In the final phases of the descent after a number of program alarms, we looked at the landing area and found a very large crater. This is the area we decided we would not go into; we extended the range downrange. The exhaust dust was kicked up by the engine and this caused some concern in that it degraded our ability to determine not only our altitude in the final phases but also our translational velocities over the ground. It's quite important not to stub your toe during the final phases of touchdown.

From the space-to-ground tapes:

EAGLE: 540 feet, down at 30 [feet per second]… down at 15…400 feet down at 9… forward… 350 feet, down at 4… 300 feet, down 3 ½… 47 forward… 1 ½ down… 13 forward… 11 forward? Coming down nicely… 200 feet, 4 ½ down… 5 ½ down… 5 percent… 75 feet… 6 forward… lights on… down 2 ½…40 feet? Down 2 ½, kicking up some dust… 30 feet, 2 ½ down… faint shadow… 4 forward… 4 forward… drifting to right a little… O.K…

HOUSTON: 30 seconds [fuel remaining].

EAGLE: Contact light! O.K., engine stops… descent engine command override off…

HOUSTON: We copy you down, Eagle.

EAGLE: Houston, Tranquility Base here. The Eagle has landed!

HOUSTON: Roger, Tranquility. We copy you on the ground. You've got a bunch of guys about to turn blue. We're breathing again. Thanks a lot.

TRANQUILITY: Thank you… That may have seemed like a very long final phase. The auto targeting was taking us right into a football-field-size crater, with a large number of big boulders and rocks for about one or two crater diameters around it, and it required flying manually over the rock field to find a reasonably good area.

HOUSTON: Roger, we copy. It was beautiful from here, Tranquility, Over.

TRANQUILITY: We'll get to the details of what's around here, but it looks like a collection of just about every variety of shape, angularity, granularity, about every variety of rock you could fine.

HOUSTON: Roger, Tranquility. Be advised there's lots of smiling faces in this room, and all over the world.

TRANQUILITY: There are two of them up here.

COLUMBIA: And don't forget one in the command module.

ARMSTRONG: Once [we] settled on the surface, the dust settled immediately and we had an excellent view of the area surrounding the LM. We saw a crater surface, pockmarked with craters up to 15, 20, 30 feet, and many smaller craters down to a diameter of 1 foot and, of course, the surface was very fine-grained. There were a surprising number of rocks of all sizes. A number of experts had, prior to flight, predicted that a good bit of difficulty might be encountered by people due to the variety of strange atmospheric and gravitational characteristics. This didn't prove to be the case and after landing we felt very comfortable in the lunar gravity. It was, in fact, in our view preferable both to weightlessness and to the earth's gravity.

When we actually descended the ladder it was found to be very much like the lunar-gravity simulations we had performed here on earth. No difficulty was encountered in descending the ladder. The last step was about 3 ½ feet from the surface, and we were somewhat concerned that we might have difficulty in reentering the LM at the end of our activity period. So we practiced that before bringing the camera down.

ALDRIN: We opened the hatch and Neil, with me as his navigator, began backing out of the tiny opening. It seemed like a small eternity before I

13

heard Neil say, "That's one small step for man... one giant leap for mankind." In less than fifteen minutes I was backing awkwardly out of the hatch and onto the surface to join Neil, who, in the tradition of all tourists, had his camera ready to photograph my arrival.

I felt buoyant and full of goose pimples when I stepped down on the surface. I immediately looked down at my feet and became intrigued with the peculiar properties of the lunar dust. If one kicks sand on a beach, it scatters in numerous directions with some grains traveling farther than others. On the moon the dust travels exactly and precisely as it goes in various directions, and every grain of it lands nearly the same distance away.

The Boy in the Candy Store:

ARMSTRONG: There were a lot of things to do, and we had a hard time getting, things finished. We had very little trouble, much less trouble than expected, on the surface. It was a pleasant operation. Temperatures weren't high. They were very comfortable. The little EMU, the combination of spacesuit and backpack that sustained our life on the surface, operated magnificently. The primary difficulty was just far too little time to do the variety of things we would have liked. We had the problem of the five-year-old boy in a candy store

ALDRIN: I took off jogging to test my maneuverability. The exercise gave me an odd sensation and looked even odder when I later saw the films of it. With bulky suits on, we seemed to be moving in slow motion. I noticed immediately that my inertia seemed much greater. Earth-bound, I would have stopped my run in just one step, but I had to use three of four steps to sort of wind down. My earth weight, with the big backpack and heavy suit, was 360 pounds. On the moon I weighed only 60 pounds.

At one point I remarked that the surface was "Beautiful, beautiful. Magnificent desolation." I was struck by the contrast between the starkness of the shadows and the desert-like barrenness of the rest of the surface. It ranged from dusty gray to light tan and was unchanging except for one startling sight: our LM sitting there with its black, silver, and bright yellow-orange thermal coating was shining brightly in the otherwise colorless landscape. I had seen Neil in his suit thousands of times before, but on the moon the unnatural whiteness of it seemed unusually brilliant. We could also look around and see earth, which, though much larger than the moon the earth was seeing, seemed small—a beckoning oasis shining far away in the sky.

As the sequence of lunar operations evolved, Neil had the camera most of the time and the majority of pictures taken on the moon that include an astronaut are of me. It wasn't until we were back on earth and in the Lunar Receiving Laboratory looking over the pictures that we realized there were few pictures of Neil. My fault perhaps, but we had never simulated this in our training.

Coaxing the Flag to Stand:

During a pause in experiments, Neil suggested we proceed with the flag. It took both of us to set it up and it was nearly a disaster. Public Relations obviously needed practice just as everything else does. A small telescoping arm was attached to the flagpole to keep the flag extended and perpendicular. As hard as we tried, the telescope wouldn't fully extend. Thus the flags which should have been flat had their own unique permanent wave. Then to our dismay the staff of the pole wouldn't go far enough into the lunar surface to support itself in an upright, but in a most precarious position. I dreaded the possibility of the American flag collapsing into the lunar dust in front of the television camera.

COLLINS: [On his fourth orbital pass above] "How's it going?" "The EVA is progressing beautifully. I believe they're setting up the flag now." Just let things keep going that way, and no surprises, please. Neil and Buzz sound good, with no huffing and puffing to indicate they are overexerting themselves. But one surprise at least is in store. Houston comes on the air, not the slightest bit ruffled, and announces that the President of the United States would like to talk to Neil and Buzz. "That would be an honor," says Neil, with characteristic dignity.

The President's voice smoothly fills the air waves with the unaccustomed cadence of the speechmaker, trained to convey inspiration, or at least emotion, instead of our usual diet of numbers and reminders. "Neil and Buzz, I am talking to you by telephone from the Oval Office at the White House, and this certainly has to be the most historic telephone call ever made… Because of what you have done, the havens have become a part of man's world. As you talk to us from the Sea of Tranquility, it inspires us to redouble our efforts to bring peace and tranquility to earth…" My God, I never thought of all this bringing peace and tranquility to anyone. As far as I am concerned, this voyage is fraught with hazards for the three of us and especially two of us and that is about as far as I have gotten in my thinking.

Neil, however, pauses long enough to give as well as he receives. "It's a great honor and privilege for us to be here, representing not only the United States but men of peace of all nations, and with interest and a curiosity and a vision for the future." [Later] Houston cuts off the White House and returns to business as usual, with a long string of numbers for me to copy for future use. My God, the juxtaposition of the incongruous-roll, pitch, and yaw was prayers, peace, and tranquility. What will be like if we really carry this off and return to earth in one peace, with our boxes full of rocks and our heads full of new perspectives for the planet? I have a little time to ponder this as I zing off out of sight of the White House and the earth.

ALDRIN: We had a pulley system to load on the boxes of rocks. We found the process more time-consuming and dust scattering than anticipated. After the gear and both of us were inside, our first chore was to pressure the LM cabin and begin stowing the rock boxes, film magazines, and anything else we wouldn't need until we were connected once again with Columbia. We removed our boots and the big backpacks, opened the LM hatch, and threw these items onto the lunar surface, along with a bagful of empty food packages and the LM urine bags. The exact moment we tossed every thing

16

out was measured back on earth the seismometer we had put out was even more sensitive than we had expected.

Before beginning liftoff procedures [we] settled down for our fitful rest. We didn't sleep much at all. Among other things we were elated and also cold. Liftoff from the moon, after a stay totaling twenty-one hours, was concentrating on the ascent engine. There was no time to sightsee. I was concentrating on the computers, and Neil was studying the attitude indicator, but I looked up long enough to see the flag fall over... Three hours and ten minutes later we were connected once again with Columbia.

COLLINS: I can look out through my docking reticle and see that they are steady as a rock as they drive down the center line of that final approach path. I gave them some numbers. "I have 0.7 mile and I got you at 31 feet per second." We really are going to carry this off for the first time since I was assigned to this incredible flight, I feel that it is going to happen. Granted, we are a long way from home, but from here on it should be all downhill. Within a few seconds Houston joins the conversation, with a tentative little call. "Eagle and Columbia, Houston standing by." They want to know what the hell is going on, but they don't want to interrupt us if we are in a crucial spot in our final maneuvering. Good heads! However, they needn't worry, and Neil lets them know it. "Roger, we're station-keeping."

All Smiles and Giggles:

[After docking] it's time to hustle down into the tunnel and remove hatch, probe, and drogue, so Neil and Buzz can get through. Thank God, all the claptraps work beautifully in this its final workout. The probe and drogue will stay with the LM and be abandoned with it, for we will have no further need of them and don't want them cluttering up command module. The first one through is Buzz, with a big smile on his face. I grab his head, a hand on each temple, and am about to give him a smooch on the forehead, as a parent might greet an errant child; but then, embarrassed, I think better of it and grab his hand, and then Neil's. We cavort about a little bit, all smiles and a giggle over our success, and then it's back to work as usual. Excerpts from a TV program broadcast by the Apollo 11 astronauts on the last evening of the flight the day before splashdown in the Pacific:

COLLINS: "… The Saturn V rocket which put us in orbit is an incredibly complicated piece of machinery, every piece of which worked flawlessly. This computer above my head has a 38,000 word vocabulary, each word of which has been carefully chosen to be of the utmost value to us. The SPS engine, our large rocket engine on the aft end of our service module, must perform flawlessly or we would have been stranded in lunar orbit. The parachutes up above my head must work perfectly tomorrow or we will plummet into the ocean. We have always had confidence that this equipment will work properly. All this is possible only through blood, sweat, and tears of a number of people. First, there are the American workmen who put these pieces of machinery together in the factory. Secondly, there is the painstaking work done by various test teams during the assembly and retest after assembly. And finally, there are the people at Manned Spacecraft Center, both in management, in mission planning, in flight control, and last but not least, in crew training. This operation is somewhat like the periscope of a submarine. All you see is the three of us, but beneath the surface are thousands and thousands of others, and to all of those, I would like to say, "Thank you very much."

ALDRIN: "… This has been far more than three men on a mission to the moon; more, still, than the efforts of a government and industry team; more, even, than the efforts of one nation. We feel that this stands as a symbol of the insatiable curiosity of all mankind to explore the unknown. Today I feel we're really fully capable of accepting expanded roles in the exploration of space. In retrospect, we have all been particularly pleased with the call signs that we very laboriously chose for our spacecraft, Columbia and Eagle. We've been pleased with the emblem of our flight, the eagle carrying an olive branch, bringing the universal symbol of peace from the earth to the moon. Personally, in reflecting on the events of the past several days, a verse from Psalms comes to mind. "When I consider the heavens, the work of Thy fingers, the moon and stars, which Thou hast ordained; what is man that Thou art mindful of him?"

ARMSTRONG: "The responsibility for this flight lies first with history and with the giants of science who have preceded this effort; next with American people, who have, through their will, indicated their desire; next with four administrations and their Congresses, for implementing that will; and then, with the agency and industry teams that built our spacecraft, the Saturn, the Columbia, the Eagle, and the little EMU, the spacesuit and backpack that was out small spacecraft out on the lunar surface. We would like to give special thanks to all those Americans who built the spacecraft; who did the construction, design, the test, and put their hearts and all their abilities into those craft. To those people tonight, we give a special thank you, and to all the other people that are listening and watching tonight, God bless you. Good night from Apollo 11."

Apollo XI

1. Who were the crew members of the Apollo 11 mission?

2. What were the names of the backup crew members for this mission?

3. When was the Apollo 11 mission launched?

4. On what day did this mission land?

5. The duration of the Apollo 11 mission was?

6. What was the mission objective for this mission?

7. The mission highlights for the Apollo 11 mission were?

8. Which astronaut took most of the pictures on this mission?

9. What was the name on the sea on the moon?

10. Did any problems occur while raising our flag?

11. Which aircraft carrier was used to pick up the astronauts and spaceship?

12. What did the inscription on the plaque say?

13. Astronauts Armstrong, Aldrin and Copper received what medal for President Nixon?

14. The computer used in the Saturn V rocket had how many words installed into it?

15. What were the last 8 words said by Armstrong before entering into the ocean?

Crew:

        Charles Conrad, Jr.
        Richard F. Gordon
        Alan L. Bean

Launch:

        November 14, 1969.

Orbit:

        Orbits: 45
        Duration: 10 days, 4 hours, 36 minutes
        Lunar Location: Ocean of Storms
        Lunar coords: 3.04 degrees south, 23.42 degrees west

Landing:

November 24, 1969.

Mission Highlights:

Landing site was the Ocean of Storms. Its mission was to retrieved parts of the unmanned Surveyor 3, which had landed on the moon in April 1967. Apollo Lunar Surface Experiments Package (ALSP) deployed. Lunar surface stay time was, 31.5 hours; in lunar orbit 89 hours, with 45 orbits. LM descent stage impacted on moon. 34kg (75lbs) of material gathered.

Apollo XII

1. Who was the crew of Apollo 12 mission?

2. Was there a backup crew on this mission?

3. What was the launch date for the Apollo 12 mission?

4. On what day did this mission land?

5. What was the duration of the Apollo 12 mission?

6. How many orbits did this mission have?

7. What was the lunar location of the Apollo 12 mission?

8. How long did this mission stay on the lunar surface?

9. What was the mission highlights of the Apollo 12 mission?

10. What does ALSEP stand for?

Crew:

James A. Lovell, Jr.
John L. Swigert
Fred W. Haise, Jr.

Mission Objective:

Apollo 13 was supposed to land in the Fra Mauro area. An explosion on board forced Apollo 13 to circle the moon without landing. The Fra Mauro site was reassigned to Apollo 14.

Launch:

Was Saturday, April 11, 1970 at 13:13 CST.

1

At five and a half minutes after liftoff, Swigert, Haise and Lovell felt a little vibration. Then the center engine of the S-II stage shut down two minutes early. This caused the remaining four engines to burn 34 seconds longer than planned, and the S-IVB third stage had to burn nine seconds longer to put Apollo 13 in orbit

Days before the mission, backup LM pilot Charlie Duke inadvertently exposed the crew to German measles. Command module pilot, Ken Mattingly, turned out to have no immunity to measles and was replaced by backup command module pilot Jack Swigert.

Ground tests before launch, indicated the possibility of a poorly insulated supercritical helium tank in the LM's descent stage so the flight plan was modified to enter the LM three hours early in order to obtain an onboard readout of helium tank pressure.

The No.2 oxygen tank, serial number 10024X-TA0009 had been previously installed in the service module of Apollo 10, but was removed for modification (and was damaged in the process of removal). The tank was fixed, tested at the Factory, installed in the Apollo 13 service module, and tested again during the Countdown Demonstration Test (CDT) at the Kennedy Space Center, beginning March 16, 1970. The tanks normally are emptied to about half full, and No. 1 behaved all right. But No.2 dropped to only 92 percent of capacity. Gaseous oxygen at 80 psi was applied through the vent line to expel the liquid oxygen, but to no avail. An interim discrepancy report was written, and on March 27, two weeks before launch, detanking operations were resumed. No. 1 again emptied normally, but No. 2 did not. After a conference with contractor and NASA personnel, the test director decided to "boil off" the remaining oxygen in No. 2 by using the electrical heater within the tank. The technique worked, but it took eight hours of 65-volt DC power from the ground support equipment to dissipate the oxygen. Due to an oversight in replacing an underrated component during a design modification, this turned out to severely damage the internal heating elements of the tank.

Orbit:

Duration: 5 days, 22 hours, 54minutes.
Lunar Location: none
Lunar Coords: none

Landing:

April 17, 1970

Mission Highlights:

Third lunar landing attempt mission was aborted after rupture of service module oxygen tank. This mission was classed as a "successful failure" because of experience in rescuing crew. Spent upper stage successfully impacted on the moon.

The first two days the crew ran into a couple of minor surprises, but generally Apollo 13was looking like the smoothest flight of the program. At 46 hours 43 minutes Joe Kerwin, the CapCom on duty, said, " The spacecraft is in real good shape as far as we are concerned. We're bored to tears down here." It was the last time anyone would mention boredom for a long time.

At 55 hours 46 minutes, as the crew finished a 49 minute TV broadcast showing how comfortably they lived and worked in weightlessness, Lovell stated: "This is the crew of Apollo 13 wishing everybody there a nice evening, and we're just about ready to close out our inspection of Aquarius (the LM) and get back for a pleasant evening in Odyssey (the CM) Good night."

Nine minutes later, Oxygen tank No. 2 blew up, causing No.1 tank to also fail. The Apollo 13 command modules normal supply of electricity, light, and water was lost, and they were about 200,000 miles from earth.

The message came in the form of a sharp bang and vibration. Jack Swigert saw a warning light that accompanied the bang, and said, "Houston, we've had a problem here." Lovell came on and told the ground that it was a main B bus under-volt. The time was 2108 hours on Apollo 13.

Next, the warning lights indicated the loss of two of Apollo 13's three fuel cells, which were the spacecrafts prime source of electricity. With warning lights blinking on, one oxygen tank appeared to be completely empty, and there were indications that the oxygen in the second tank was rapidly being depleted. Thirteen minutes after the explosion, Lovell happened to look out of the left-hand window, and saw the final evidence pointing toward potential catastrophe. "We are venting something out into the- into space," he reported to Houston. Jack Lousma, the CapCom replied, "Roger, we copy you venting." Lovell said, "It's a gas of some sort." It was oxygen gas escaping at a high rate from the second, and last, oxygen tank.

The first thing the crew did, even before discovering the oxygen leak, was to try to close the hatch between the CM and the LM. They reacted spontaneously, like submarine crews, closing the hatch, but the stubborn lid wouldn't stay shut. Exasperated, and realizing that there wasn't a cabin leak, they strapped the hatch to the CM couch.

The pressure in the No. 1 oxygen tank continued to drift downward; passing 300 psi, now heading toward 200 psi. Months later, after the accident investigation was complete, it was determined that, when No. 2 tank blew up, it either ruptured a line on the No. 1 tank, or caused one of the valves to leak. When the pressure reached 200 psi, the crew and ground controllers knew that they would lose all oxygen, which meant that the last fuel cell would also die.

At 1 hour and 29 seconds after the bang, Jack Lousma, then CapCom, said after instructions from flight Director Glynn Lunney: "It is slowly going to zero, and we are starting to think about the LM lifeboat." Swigert replied, "That's what we have been thinking about too."

Ground controllers in Houston faced a formidable task. Completely new procedures had to be written and tested in the simulator before being passed up to the crew. The navigation problem had to be solved; essentially how, when, and in what attitude to burn the LM descent engine to provide a quick return home. With only 15 minutes of power left in the CM, CapCom told the crew to make their way into the LM. Fred and Jim Lovell quickly floated through the tunnel, leaving Jack to perform the last chores in the Command Module. The first concern was to determine if there were enough consumables to get home? The LM was built for only a 45 hour lifetime, and it needed to be stretch to 90.

Oxygen wasn't a problem. The full LM descent tank alone would suffice, and in addition, there were two ascent-engine oxygen tanks, and two backpacks whose oxygen supply would never be used on the lunar surface. Two emergency bottles on top of those packs had six or seven pounds each in them. (At LM jettison, just before reentry, 28.5 pounds of oxygen remained, more than half of what was available after the explosion).

Power was also a concern. Then were 2181 ampere hours in the LM batteries, Ground controllers carefully worked out a procedure where the CM batteries were charged with LM power. All non-critical systems were turned off and energy consumption was reduced to a fifth of normal, which resulted in having 20 percent of our LM electrical power left when Aquarius was jettisoned. There was one electrical close call during the mission. One of the CM batteries vented with such force that it momentarily dropped off the line. Had the battery failed, there would be insufficient power to return the ship to earth.

Water was the main consumable concern. It was estimated that the crew would run out of water about five hours before earth reentry, which was calculated at around 151 hours. However, data from Apollo 11 (which had not sent its LM ascent stage crashing into the moon as in subsequent missions) showed that its mechanisms could survive seven or eight hours in space without water cooling. The crew conserved water. They cut down to six ounces each per day, a fifth of normal intake, and used fruit juices; they ate hot dogs and other wet-pack foods when they ate at all. The crew became dehydrated throughout the flight and set a record that stood up throughout Apollo: Lovell lost fourteen pounds, and the crew lost a total of 31.5 pounds, nearly 50 percent more than any other crew. Those stringent measures resulted in the crew finishing with 28.2 pounds of water, about 9 percent of the total.

Removal of Carbon Dioxide was also a concern. There were enough lithium hydroxide canisters, which remove carbon dioxide from the spacecraft, but the square canisters from the Command Module were not compatible with the round openings in the Lunar Module environmental system. There were four cartridges from the LM, and four from the backpacks, counting backups. However, the LM was designed to support two men for two days and was being asked to care for three men nearly four days. After a day and a half in the LM a warning light showed that the carbon dioxide had built up to a dangerous level. Mission Control devised a way to attach the CM canisters to the LM system by using plastic bags, cardboard, and tape all materials carried on board.

One of the biggest questions was, "How to get back safely to earth?" The LM navigation system wasn't designed to help us in this situation. Before the explosion, at 30 hours and minutes, Apollo 13 had made the normal midcourse correction, which would take it out of a free return to earth trajectory and put it on a lunar landing course. Now the task was to get back on a free return course. The ground computed a 35 second burn and fired it 5 hours after the explosion. As they approached the moon, another burn was computed; this time a long 5 minute burn to speed up the return home. It took place 2 hours after rounding the far side of the moon.

The Command Module navigational platform alignment was transferred to the LM but verifying alignment was difficult. Ordinarily the alignment procedure uses an onboard sextant device, called the Alignment Optical Telescope, to find a suitable navigation star. Then with the help of the onboard computer verify the guidance platform's alignment. However, due to the explosion, a swarm of debris from the ruptured service module made it impossible to sight real stars. An alternated procedure was developed to use the sun as an alignment star. Lovell rotated the spacecraft to attitude Houston had requested and when he looked through the AOT, the sun was just where it was expected. The alignment with the sun proved to be less than a half a degree off. The ground and crew then knew they could do the 5 minute P.C. + 2 burns with assurance, and that would cut the total time of voyage to about 142 hours. At 73:46 hours the air to ground transcript describes the event:

Lovell: O.K. We got it. I think we got it. What diameter was it?

Haise: Yes. It's coming back in. Just about it.

Lovell: Yes, yaw's coming back in. Just about it.

Haise: Yaw is in….

Lovell: What have you got?

Haise: Upper right corner of the sun….

Lovell: We've got it!

If we raised our voices, I submit it was justified.

"I'm told the cheer of the year went up in Mission Control." Flight Director Gerald Griffin, a man not easily shaken, recalls: "Some years later I went back to the log and looked up that mission. My writing was almost illegible I was so damned nervous. And I remember the exhilaration running through me: My God, that's kinds the last hurdle – if we can do that, I know we can make it. It was funny, because only the people involved knew how important it was to have that platform properly aligned." Yet Gerry Griffin barely mentioned the alignment in his change-of-shift briefing – "That check turned out real well" is all he said an hour after his penmanship failed him.

The trip was marked by discomfort beyond the lack of food and water. Sleep was almost impossible because of the cold. When the electrical system was turned off, the spacecraft lost and important source of heat. The temperature dropped to 38 degrees F and condensation formed on all the walls.

A most remarkable achievement of Mission Control was quickly developing procedures for powering up the CM after its long cold sleep. Flight controllers wrote the documents for this innovation in three days, instead of the usual three months. The Command Module was cold and clammy at the start of power up. The walls, ceiling, floor, wire harnesses, and panels were all covered with droplets of water. It was suspected conditions were the same behind the panels. The chances of short circuits caused apprehension, but thanks to the safeguards built into the command module after the disastrous Apollo 1 fire in January 1967, no arcing took place. The droplets furnished one sensation as we decelerated in the atmosphere: it rained inside the CM.

Four hours before landing, the crew shed the service module; Mission Control had insisted on retaining it until then because everyone feared what the cold of space might do to the unsheltered CM heat shield. Photos of the Service Module showed one whole panel missing, and wreckage hanging out, it was a sorry mess as it drifted away. Three hours later the crew left the Lunar Module Aquarius and then splashed down gently in the Pacific Ocean near Samoa.

After an intensive investigation, the Apollo13 Accident Review Board identified the cause of the explosion. In 1965 the CM had undergone many improvements, which included raising the permissible voltage to the heaters in the oxygen tanks from 28 to 65 volts DC. Unfortunately, the thermostatic switches on these heaters weren't modified to suit the change. During one final test on the launch pad, the heaters were on for a long period of time. "This subjected the wiring in the vicinity of the heaters to very high temperatures (1000F), which have been subsequently shown to severely degrade Teflon insulation. The thermostatic switches started to open while powered by 65 volts DC and were probably welded shut." Furthermore, other warning signs during testing went unheeded and the tank, damaged from 8 hours overheating, was a potential bomb the next time it was filled with oxygen. That bomb exploded on April 13, 1970 200,000 miles from earth.

Apollo XIII

1. Who were the crew members of the Apollo 13?

2. Was there a backup crew for this mission?

3. What was the launch date for the Apollo 13?

4. On what date did this mission landed?

5. The Apollo 13 was supposed to land where?

6. What happened on this mission to cause the Apollo 13 to circle the moon without landing?

7. The mission objectives for the Apollo 13 were what?

8. What was the duration of this mission?

9. Did any mishaps occur on this mission? If so what were they?

10. What was the mission highlights for the Apollo 13 mission?

Bonus: The Fra Mauro landing site was reassigned to what mission?

Crew:

Alan B. Shepard, Jr.
Stuart A. Roosa
Edgar D. Mitchell

Launch:

January 31, 1971

Orbit:

Orbits: 34
Duration: 9 days
Lunar Location: Fra Mauro
Lunar Coords: 3.65 degrees south, 17.48 degrees west.

1

Landing:

February 9, 1971

Mission Highlights:

Landing site was on Fra Mauro. ALSEP and other instruments deployed. Lunar surface stay-time was, 33.5 hours; 67 hours in lunar orbit, with 34 orbits. 2 EVAs were 9 hours, 25 minutes. Third stage impacted on the moon. 42 kg (94 lbs) of materials was gathered, using hand cart for the first time to transport rocks.

Apollo XIV

1. Who were the crew members on the Apollo 14 mission?

2. Was there a backup crew for this mission? If so who were they?

3. What was the date that the Apollo 14 mission was launched?

4. How many orbits did this mission have?

5. What was the duration of the Apollo 14 mission?

6. The lunar location was where for this mission?

7. What were the lunar coords for the Apollo 14 mission?

8. On what day did this mission land?

9. What was the mission highlights for the Apollo 14 mission?

10. How much materials were gathered by the hand carton this mission?

Crew:

David R. Scott
James B. Irwin
Alfred M. Worden

Launch:

July 26, 1971

Orbit:

Orbits: 74
Duration: 12 days, 17 hours, 12 minutes
Lunar Location: Hadley-Apennine
Lunar Coords: 26.08 degrees north, 3.66 degrees east.

1

Landing:

August 7, 1971

Mission Highlights:

Landing site: was Hadley-Apennine region, near Apennine Mountains. 3 EVAs were 10 hours, 36 minutes. Worden performed 38 minutes of EVAs on the way back to earth. This mission was the first to carry orbital sensors in service module of CSM. ALSEP deployed. Scientific payload landed on moon doubled. Improved spacesuits gave increased mobility and stay-time. Lunar surface stay-time was 66.9 hours. Lunar Roving Vehicle (LRV), electric powered, 4-wheel drive car, traversed total 27.9 km (17 miles). They spent 145 hours in lunar orbit, with 74 orbits. Small sub-satellite left in lunar orbit for first time. 6.6 kg (169 lbs) of material gathered.

Apollo XV

1. Who were the crew members of Apollo 15?

2. Was there a backup crew for this mission?

3. What was the date that Apollo 15 was launched?

4. On what date did this mission land?

5. How many orbits did the Apollo 15 mission have?

6. What was the duration of this mission?

7. Where was the lunar location for the Apollo 15?

8. What were the lunar coords for this mission?

9. The mission highlights for the Apollo 15 were?

10. What was the lunar surface stay-time?

Crew:

John W. Young
Thomas K. Mattingly, II
Charles M. Duke, Jr.

Launch:

April 16, 1972

Orbit:

Orbits: 64
Duration: 11 days, 1 hour, 51 minutes.
Lunar Location: Descartes Highlands
Lunar Coords: 8.97 degrees south, 15.51 degrees east

Landing:

April 27, 1972

Mission Highlights:

The landing site was Descartes Highlands. This was the first study of the highlands area. Selected surface experiments deployed, ultraviolet camera/spectrograph was used for the first time on the moon, and LRV was used for the second time. They stayed on the lunar surface for, 71 hours; and in lunar orbit for 126 hours, with 64 orbits. Mattingly performed; 1 hour of in-flight EVA. 95.8 kg (213 lbs) of lunar samples were collected.

Apollo XVI

1. Who were the crew members on the Apollo 16 mission?

2. Was there any backup crew members for this mission?

3. What was the Launch date for the Apollo 16?

4. How many orbits did this mission have?

5. What was the duration of the Apollo 16 mission?

6. Where was the lunar location for this mission?

7. What were the lunar coords for Apollo 16?

8. How many hours did this mission stay in orbit?

9. On what date did the Apollo 16 land?

10. The mission highlights for this mission were?

Crew:

Eugene A. Cernan: Commander
Ronald E. Evans: Command Module Pilot
Harrison H. Schmitt: Lunar Module Pilot

Mission Objective:

The Lunar landing site was the Taurus-Littrow highlands and valley area. This site was picked for Apollo 17 as a location where rocks both older and younger than those previously returned from other Apollo missions and from the Luna 16 and 20 missions might be found.

The mission was the final in a series of three J-type missions planned for the Apollo program. These J-type missions can be distinguished from previous G and H-series missions by extended hardware capability, larger scientific payload capacity and by the use of battery powered Lunar Roving Vehicle (LRV).

Scientific objectives of the Apollo 17 mission included geological surveying and sampling of materials and surface features in a preselected area of the Taurus-Littrow region, deploying and activating surface experiments, and conducting in-flight experiments and photographic tasks during lunar orbit and transearth coast (TEC). These objectives included: Deployed experiments such as the Apollo lunar surface experiment package (ALSEP) with a Heat Flow experiment, Lunar seismic profiling (LSP), Lunar surface gravimeter (LSG), Lunar atmospheric composition experiment (LACE) and Lunar ejecta and meteorites (LEAM). The mission also included Lunar Sampling and Lunar orbital experiments. Biomedical experiments included the Biostack II Experiment and the BIOCORE experiment.

Launch:

Apollo 17 was launched on December 7, 1972, at 12:33:00 a.m. EST from Kennedy Space Center. The CSM, LM and SIVB booster stage were inserted 11 minutes 53 seconds after launch into an earth parking orbit of 91.2 by 92.5 n. mi. After two revolutions, at 8:45:37 GMT, Apollo 17 was inserted into translunar coast.

Orbit:

Duration: 12 days, 13 hours, 52minutes.
Surface-Time: 75 hours.
Lunar Location: Taurus-Littrow.
Lunar Coords: 20.16 degrees north, 30.77 degrees east.

Landing:

December 19, 1972

Mission highlights:

At 9:15:29 GMT on December 7, 1972, the CSM was separated from the SIVB. Approximately15 minutes later, the CSM docked with the LM. After CSM/LM extraction from the SIVB, the SIVB was targeted for lunar impact, which occurred on December 10 at 20:32:43 GMT. The impact location was approximately 84nm northwest of the planned target point and the event was recorded by the passive seismic experiments deployed on the Apollo 12, apollo14, apollo15 and apollo16 missions.

Only one of the four planned midcourse corrections was required during translunar coast. A midcourse correction made at 17:03:00 GMT on December 8, 1927 was a 1.6 sec service propulsion system burn resulting in a 10>: 5 ft/sec velocity change. Lunar orbit insertion was accomplished at 19:47:23 GMT on December 10, 1972 placing the spacecraft into a lunar orbit of 170nm by 52.6nm. Approximately 4 hours 20 minutes later, the orbit was reduced to 59nm by 15nm. The spacecraft remained in this low orbit for more than 18 hours, during which time the CMS/LM undocking and separation were performed. The CSM circularization maneuver was performed at 18:50:29 GMT on December 11, 1972 which placed the CSM into an orbit of 70.3nm by 54.3nm. At 14:35:00 GMT on December 11, 1972, the Commander and Lunar Module Pilot entered the LM to prepare for descent to the lunar surface. At 18:55:42 GMT on December 11, 1972, the LM was placed into an orbit with a perilune altitude of 6.2nm. Approximately 47 minutes later, the powered descent to the lunar surface began. Landing occurred at 19:54:57 GMT on December 11, 1972 at lunar latitude 20 degrees 10 minutes north and longitude 30 degrees 46 minutes east.

Apollo 17 was the last lunar landing mission. There were 3 EVAs of 22 hours, 4 minutes on the lunar surface. EVA#1 began at 23:54:49 GMT on December 11, 1972 with Cernan egressing at 00:01:00 GMT on December 12, 1972. The 1st EVA was 7 hours 12 minutes long and was completed at 7:06:42 GMT on December 12, 1972. The second EVA was begun at 23:28:06 GMT on December 12, 1972. It lasted 7 hours 37 minutes and ended at 7:05:02 GMT on December 13, 1972. The final EVA began at 22:25:48 GMT on December 13, 1972 and ended at 5:40:56 GMT on December 14, 1972.

The LM ascent stage lifted off the moon at 22:54:37 GMT on December 14, 1972. After a vernier adjustment maneuver, the ascent stage was inserted into a 48.5nm by 9.4 nm orbit. The LM terminal phase initiation burn was made at 23:48:58 GMT on December 14, 1972. This 3.2 second maneuver raised the ascent stage orbit to 64.7nm by 48.5nm. The CSM and LM docked at 1:10:15 GMT. The LM ascent stage was jettisoned at 4:51:31 GMT on December 15, 1972. Deorbit firing of the ascent stage was initiated at 6:31:14 GMT on December 15, 1972 and lunar impact occurred 19

3

minutes 07 seconds later approximately 0.7nm from planned target at latitude 19 degrees 56 minutes north and longitude 30 degrees 32 minutes east. The ascent stage impact was recorded by the four Apollo 17 geophones and by each ALSEP at Apollo 12, Apollo14, Apollo 15 and Apollo 16 landings sites.

Evans performed a trans-earth EVA at 20:27:40 GMT on December 17, 1972, lasting 1 hour 6minutes during which time the CMP retrieved the lunar sounder film and the panoramic and mapping camera film cassettes.

Apollo 17 hosted the first scientist- astronaut to land on the moon, Schmitt. Sixth automated research station was set up. LRV traverse total 30.5 km. Lunar surface stay-time, 75 hours. In lunar orbit was 17 hours. 110.4 kg (234lbs) of material gathered.

Apollo XVII

1. Who were the crew members of the Apollo 17 mission?

2. Where was the lunar landing site for this mission?

3. Why was this site chosen for the Apollo 17 mission?

4. What was the launch date for this mission?

5. On what date did the Apollo 17 land?

6. What was the mission objective for this mission?

7. The duration of the Apollo 17 mission was for how long?

8. At what date and time did lunar impact occur on this mission?

9. How long did it take the Apollo 17 mission to complete the 3 EVAs?

10. What was the mission highlights for this mission?

NEIL A. ARMSTRONG NASA ASTRONAUT (former)

PERSONAL DATA: Born August 5, 1930 in Wapakoneta, Ohio. He is married with two sons.

EDUCATION: Bachelor of Science degree in aeronautical engineering from Purdue University; Master of Science Degree in aeronautical engineering from University of Southern California. He holds honorary doctorates from a number of universities.

SPECIAL HONORS: He is the recipient of many special honors, including the P residential Medal for Freedom in 1969; the Robert H. Goddard Memorial Trophy in 1970; the Robert J. Collier Trophy in 1969; and the congressional Space Medal of Honor, 1978.

NASA EXPERIENCE: Armstrong joined NACA, (National Advisory Committee for Aeronautics), NASA's predecessor, as a research pilot at the Lewis Laboratory in Cleveland and later transferred to the NACA High Speed Flight Station at Edwards AFB, California. He was a project pilot on many pioneering high speed aircraft, including jets, rockets, helicopters and gliders.

In 1962, Armstrong was transferred to astronaut status. He served as command pilot for the Gemini 8 mission, launched March 16, 1966, and performed the first successful docking of two vehicles in space.

In 1969, Armstrong was commander of Apollo 11, the first manned lunar landing mission, and gained the distinction of being the first man to land a craft on the moon and the first man step on its surface.

Armstrong subsequently held the position of Deputy Associate Administrator for Aeronautics, NASA Headquarters Office of Advanced Research and Technology, from 1970 to 1971. He resigned from NASA in 1971.

Frank Borman

A hero of the American Space Odyssey, Frank Borman led the first team of American astronauts to circle the moon, extending man's horizons into space. He is internationally known as Commander of the 1968 Apollo 8 Mission. A romance with airplanes that began when he was 15 years old, took Frank Borman to the Air Force and then to NASA.

A career Air Force officer from 1950, his assignments included service as a fighter pilot, an operational pilot and instructor, an experimental test pilot and an assistant professor of Thermodynamics and Fluid Mechanics at West Point. When selected by NASA, Frank Borman was instructor at the Aerospace Research Pilot School at Edwards AFB, California.

In 1967 he served as a member of the Apollo 204 Fire Investigation Board, investigating the causes of the fire which killed three astronauts aboard an Apollo spacecraft, reminiscent of the Challenger tragedy. Later he became the Apollo Program Resident Manager, heading the team that re-engineered the Apollo spacecraft. He also served as Field Director of NASA's Space Station Task Force.

Frank Borman retired from the Air Force in 1970, but is well remembered as a part of this nation's history, a pioneer in the exploration of space and a veteran of both the Gemini 7, 1965 Space Orbital Rendezvous with Gemini 6 and the first manned lunar orbital mission, Apollo 8, in 1968.

He received the Congressional Space Medal of Honor from the President of the United States. Colonel Borman also was awarded the Harmon International Aviation Trophy, the Robert J. Collier Trophy, the Tony Jannus Award and the National Geographic Society's Hubbard Medal, in addition to many honorary degrees, special honors and service decorations. More recently, in September of 1990, Colonel Broman along with fellow Apollo 8 astronauts, Lovell and Anders, was inducted into the International Aerospace Hall of Fame, and in October of 1990 received the Airport Operators Council International Downes Award. In March 1993, he was inducted into the U.S. Astronaut Hall of Fame.

Frank Borman was born in Gary, Indiana, and raised in Tucson, Arizona. He earned a Bachelor of Science degree from the U.S. Military Academy, West Point, in 1950 and a Master of Science degree in Aeronautical Engineering from the California Institute of Technology in 1957. He completed the Harvard Business School's Advanced Management Program in 1970.

M. Scott Carpenter

Original Mercury 7 Astronaut: Scott Carpenter, a dynamic pioneer of modern exploration, has the unique distinction of being the first human ever to penetrate both inner and outer space, thereby acquiring the dual title, Astronaut/Aquanaut.

He was born in Boulder, Colorado, on May 1, 1925, the son of research chemist Dr. M. Scott Carpenter and Florence Kelso Noxon Carpenter. He attended the University of Colorado from 1945 to 1949 and received a Bachelor of Science degree in Aeronautical Engineering.

Carpenter was commissioned in the U.S. Navy in 1949. He was given flight training at Pensacola, Florida and Corpus Christi, Texas and designated a Naval Aviator in April, 1951. During the Korean War he served with patrol Squadron Six, flying antisubmarine, ship surveillance, and aerial mining, and ferret missions in the Yellow Sea, South China Sea, and the Formosa Straits.

From 1957 to 1959 he attended the Navy General Line School and the Navy Air Intelligence School and was then assigned as Air Intelligence Officer to the Aircraft Carrier, USS Hornet. Carpenter was selected as one of the original seven Mercury Astronauts on April 9, 1959. He underwent intensive training with the

National Aeronautics and Space Administration (NASA), specializing in communication and navigation. He served as backup pilot for John Glenn during the preparation for America's first manned orbital space flight in February 1962.

Carpenter flew the second American manned orbital flight on May 24, 1962. He piloted his Aurora 7 spacecraft through three revolutions of the earth, reaching a maximum altitude of 164 miles. The spacecraft landed in the Atlantic Ocean about 1000 miles southeast of Cape Canaveral after 4 hours and 54 minutes of flight time.

CHARLES CONRAD, JR., (CAPTIN, USN, RET.) NASA ASTRONAUT (DECEASED)

PERSONAL DATA: Born June 2, 1930, in Philadelphia, Pennsylvania. Died July 8, 1999, from injuries sustained in a motorcycle accident in Ojai, California. Conrad, who divorced his first wife, is survived by his wife Nancy, three sons and seven grandchildren. A son preceded him in death.

EDUCATION: Attended primary and secondary schools at Haverford School in Haverford, Pennsylvania, and the Darrow School, New Lebanon, New York; received a Bachelor of Science degree in Aeronautical Engineering from Princeton University in 1970, and an honorary doctorate of science degree from king's college, Wilkes-Barre, Pennsylvania in 1971.

AEROSPACE EXPERIENCE: In September of 1962, Mr. Conrad was selected as an astronaut by NASA. His first flight was Gemini V, which established the space endurance record and placed the United States in the lead for man-hours in space. As commander of Gemini XI, Mr. Conrad helped to set a world's altitude record. He then served as commander of Apollo XII, the second lunar landing. On Mr. Conrad's final mission, he served as commander of Skylab II, the first United States Space Station.

In December 1973, after serving 20 years (11 of which were as an astronaut in the space program).

In 1990, Mr.Conrad became Staff Vice President of New Business for McDonell Douglas Space Company, where he participated in research and development for the Space Exploration Initiative. Included for research and development in the Space Exploration Initiative are the construction of Space Station Freedom, the return to and colonization of the moon, and the exploration of Mars. Mr. Conrad contributed his expertise on SSTO, the Single-Stage-To-Orbit and return space transportation system called the Delta Clipper. In 1993, Mr. Conrad become Vice President-Project Development.

L. Gordon Cooper Jr.:

Original Mercury 7 Astronaut

PERSONAL DATA: Born March 6, 1927 in Shawnee, Oklahoma.

EDUCATION: Attended primary and secondary schools in Shawnee, Oklahoma and Murray, Kentucky; received a Bachelor of Science degree in Aeronautical Engineering from the Air Force Institute of Technology (AFIT) in 1956; recipient of an Honorary Doctorate of Science Degree from Oklahoma City University in 1967.

NASA EXPERIENCE: Colonel Cooper was selected as a Mercury astronaut in April 1959.

On May 15-16, 1963, he piloted the "Faith 7" spacecraft on a 22-orbit mission which concluded the operational phase of a Project Mercury. During the 34 hours and 20 minutes of flight, Faith 7 attained an apogee of 166 statute miles and a speed of 17,546 miles per hour and traveled 546,167 statute miles.

Cooper served as command pilot of the 8 day 120 revolution Gemini 5 mission which began on August 21, 1965. It was on this flight that he and pilot Charles Conrad established a new space endurance record by traveling a distance of 3,312,933 miles in an elapsed time of 190 hours and 56 minutes. Cooper also became the first man to make a second orbital flight and thus won for the United States the lead in man-hours in space by accumulating a total of 225 hours and 15 minutes.

He served as backup command pilot for Gemini 12 and as backup commander for Apollo X.

Colonel Cooper has logged 222 hours in space.

He retired from the Air Force and NASA in 1970.

John Herschel Glenn, Jr. (Colonel, USMC, Ret.)

PERSONAL DATA: Born July 18, 1921 in Cambridge, Ohio. HE married the former Anna Margaret Castor of New Concord, Ohio. They have two grown children.

EDUCATION: Glenn attended primary and secondary schools in New Concord, Ohio. He attended Muskingum College in New Concord and received a Bachelor of Science degree in Engineering. Muskingum College also awarded him an honorary Doctor of Science degree in engineering. He has received honorary doctoral degrees from nine college or universities.

SPECIAL HONORS: Glenn has been awarded the Distinguished Flying Cross on six occasions, and holds the Air Medal with 18 clusters for his service during World War II and Korea. Glenn also holds the Navy Unit Commendation for service in Korea, the Asiatic-Pacific Campaign Medal, the American Campaign Medal, the World War II Victory Medal, the China Service Medal, the National Defense Service medal, the Korean Service Medal, the United Nations Service Medal, the Korean Presidential Unit Citation, the Navy's Astronaut Wings, the Marine Corps' Astronaut medal, the NASA Distinguished Service Medal, and the Congressional Space Medal of Honor.

NASA EXPERIENCE: Glenn was assigned to the NASA Space Task Group at Langley Research Center, Hampton, Virginia, in April 1959 after his selection as a Project Mercury Astronaut. The Space Task Group was moved to Houston and became of the NASA Manned Spacecraft Center in 1962. Glenn flew on Mercury-6 (February 20, 1962) and STS-95 (October 29 to November 7, 1998), and has logged over 218 hours in space. Prior to his first flight, Glenn had served as backup pilot for Astronauts Shepard and Grissom. When astronauts were given special assignments to ensure pilot input into the design and development of spacecraft, Glenn specialized in cockpit layout and control functioning, including some of the early designs for the Apollo Project. Glenn resigned from Manned Spacecraft Center on January 16, 1964. He was promoted to the rank of Colonel in October 1964 and retired from the Marine Corps on January 1, 1965. He was a business executive from 1965 until his election to the United States Senate in November 1974. Glenn retired from the U.S. Senate in January 1999.

SPACE FLIGHT EXPERIENCE: On February 20, 1962, Glenn piloted the Mercury-Atlas 6 "Friendship 7" spacecraft on the first manned orbital mission of the United States. Launched from Kennedy Space Center, Florida, he completed a successful three-orbit mission around the earth, reaching a maximum altitude (apogee) of approximately 162 statute miles and an orbital velocity of approximately 17, 500 miles per hour. Glenn's "Friendship 7" Mercury spacecraft landed approximately 800 miles southeast of KSC in the vicinity of Grand Turk Island. Mission duration from launch to impact was 4 hours, 55 minutes, and 23 seconds.

STS-95 Discovery (October 29 to November 7, 1998) was a 9 day mission during which the crew supported a variety of research payloads including deployment of the Spartan solar-observing spacecraft, the Hubble Space Telescope Orbital Systems Test Platform, and investigations on space flight and the aging process. The mission was accomplished in 134 earth orbits, traveling 3.6 million miles in 213 hours and 44 minutes.

Virgil I. Grissom

Original Mercury 7 Astronaut

PERSONAL DATA: Born April 3, 1926, in Mitchell, Indiana, Died January 27, 1967, at NASA Kennedy Space Center, Florida, in the Apollo 1 spacecraft fire. He is survived by his wife Betty and their two children.

EDUCATION: Graduated Mitchell High School; received a Bachelor of Science degree in Mechanical Engineering from Purdue University.

AWARDS: Posthumously awarded the Congressional Space Medal of Honor.

NASA EXPERIENCE: Grissom was one of the seven Mercury astronauts selected by NASA in April 1959. He piloted the Liberty Bell 7 spacecraft the second and final suborbital Mercury test flight on July 21, 1961. This flight lasted 15 minutes and 37 seconds, attained an altitude of 118 statute miles, and traveled 302 miles downrange from the launch pad at Cape Kennedy.

On March 23, 1965, he served as command pilot on the first manned Gemini flight, A 3 orbit mission during which the crew accomplished the first orbital trajectory modifications and the first lifting reentry of a manned spacecraft. Subsequent to this assignment, he served as backup command pilot for Gemini 6.

Grissom was named to serve as command pilot for the AS-204 mission, the first 3 man Apollo flight.

Lieutenant Colonel Grissom died on January 27, 1967, in the Apollo 1 spacecraft flash fire during a launch pad test at Kennedy Space Center, Florida.

James A. Lovell (Captain, USN, Ret.) NASA Astronaut (former)

PERSONAL DATA: Born in Cleveland, Ohio, on March 25, 1928. He married to the former Marilyn Gerlach, of Milwaukee, Wisconsin. They have four children.

EDUCATION: University of Wisconsin; United States Naval Academy, Bachelor of Science, 1952; Test Pilot School, NATC, Patuxent River, Maryland, 1958; Aviation Safety School, University of Southern California, 1961; Advanced Management Program, Harvard Business School, 1971; Honorary Doctorates from Rockhurst College, Illinois Wesleyan University, Western Michigan University, Mary Hardin-Baylor College and Milwaukee School of Engineering.

NASA EXPERIENCE: Captain Lovell was selected as an Astronaut by NASA in September 1962. He has since served as backup pilot for the Gemini 4 flight and backup Commander for the Gemini 9 flight, as well as backup Commander to Neil Armstrong for the Apollo 11 lunar landing mission.

On December 4, 1965, he and Frank Borman were launched into space on the history-making Gemini 7 mission. The flight lasted 330 hours and 35 minutes and included the first rendezvous of two manned maneuverable spacecraft.

The Gemini 12 mission, commanded by Lovell with Pilot Edwin Aldrin, began on November 11, 1966. This 4 day, 59 revolution flight brought the Gemini program to a successful close. Lovell served as Command Module Pilot and Navigator on the epic six day journey of Apollo 8 man's maiden voyage to the moon December 21-27, 1968. Apollo 8 was the first manned spacecraft to be lifted into near earth orbit by a 7 ½ million pounds thrust Saturn V launch vehicle; and Lovell and fellow crewmen, Frank Borman and William A. Anders, Became the first humans to leave the earth's gravitational influence.

He completed his fourth mission as Spacecraft Commander of the Apollo 13 flight, April 11-13, 1970, and became the first man to journey twice to the moon. Apollo 13 was programmed for ten days. However, the original flight plan was modified en route to the moon due to a failure of the Service Module cryogenic oxygen system. Lovell and fellow crewmen, John L. Swigert and Fred W. Haise, working closely with Houston ground controllers, converted their lunar module "Aquarius" into an effective lifeboat. Their emergency activation and operation of lunar module systems conserved both electrical power and water in sufficient supply to assure their safety and survival while in space and for the return to earth.

Captain Lovell held the record for time in space with a total of 715 hours and 5 minutes until surpassed by the Skylab flights.

James A. McDivitt (Brig. General, USAF Ret.) NASA Astronaut (former)

PERSON DATA: Born June 10, 1929, in Chicago, Illinois. His mother Mrs. James McDivitt resides in Jackson, Michigan. He is married with four children and two step-children.

EDUCATION: Graduated from Kalamazoo Central High School, Kalamazoo, Michigan; Jackson Junior College, Jackson, Michigan, received a Bachelor of Science degree in Aeronautical Engineering from the University of Michigan (graduated first in class) in 1959 and an Honorary Doctorate in Astronautical Science, Seton Hall University, 1969; Honorary Doctor of Science, Miami University (Ohio), 1970; Honorary Doctor of Law, Eastern Michigan University, 1975.

EXPERIENCE: McDivitt joined the Air Force in 1951 and retired with the rank of Brig. General. He flew 145 combat missions during the Korean War in F-80s and F-86s.

He is a graduate of the USAF Experimental Test Pilot School and the USAF Aerospace Research Pilot course and served as an experimental test pilot at Edwards Air Force Base, California.

He has logged over 5,000 flying hours.

NASA EXPERIENCE: General McDivitt was selected as an astronaut by NASA in September 1962.

He was command pilot for Gemini 4, a 66-orbit 4-day mission that began on June 3, and ended June 7, 1965. Highlights of the mission included a controlled extra-vehicular activity period and a number of experiments.

He was commander of Apollo 9, a 10-day earth orbital flight launched on March 3, 1969. This was the first flight of the complete set of Apollo hardware and was the first flight of the Lunar Module.

He became Manager of Lunar Landing Operations in May 1969, and led a team that planned the lunar exploration program and redesigned the spacecraft to accomplish this task. In August 1969, he became Manager of the Apollo Spacecraft Program and was the program manager for Apollo 12, 13, 14, 15, and 16.

He retired from the USAF and left NASA in June 1972.

WALTER M. SCHIRRA JR.

Original Mercury 7 Astronaut

PERSONAL DATA: Born March 12, 1923, in Hackensack, New Jersey

EDUCATION: Newark College of Engineering (N.J.I.T.), 1941; U.S. Naval Academy, 1942-1945 B.S.; Safety Officers School (U.S.C.), 1957; U.S. Navy Test Pilot School (N.A.T.C.) 1958; NASA Astronaut Training, 1959-1969; Honorary Doctorate in Astronautical Engineering, Lafayette College, 1969; Honorary Doctorate in Science, U.S.C., 1969; Honorary Doctorate in Astronautics, N.J.I.T., 1969;Trustee, Detroit Institute of Technology, 1969-1976; Advisor, Colorado State University, 1977-1982; Trustee, National College, South Dakota, 1983-1987.

AWARDS-MILITARY: U.S. Navy Distinguished Service Medal; Distinguished Flying Cross (3): Air Medal (3): NASA Distinguished Service Medal (2): NASA Exceptional Service Medal (1): Philippines Legion of Honor (Commander).

HALL OF FAME INDUCTED: International Aviation Hall of Fame, San Diego, CA, 1970; New Jersey Aviation Hall of Fame, Teterboro, NJ, 1977 (approx): International Space Hall of Fame, Alamagordo, NM, 1981; National Aviation Hall of Fame, Dayton, OH, 1986.

NASA EXPERIENCE: Captain Schirra was one of the seven Mercury Astronauts named by NASA in April 1959. On October 3, 1962; he Piloted the six orbit Sigma 7 Mercury flight; a flight which lasted 9 hours, 15 minutes. The spacecraft attained a velocity of 17,557 miles per hour at an altitude of 175 statute miles and traveled almost 144,000 statute miles before reentry into earth's atmosphere. Recovery of the Sigma 7 spacecraft occurred in the Pacific Ocean about 275 miles northeast of Midway Island.

Schirra next served as backup command pilot for the Gemini III Mission and on December 15-16, occupied the Command Pilot seat on history making Gemini 6 flight. The highlight of this mission was a successful rendezvous of Gemini 6 with the already orbiting Gemini 7 spacecraft, thus, accomplishing the first rendezvous of two manned maneuverable spacecraft and establishing another space first for the United States. Known as a "text book" pilot, Schirra remained in the spacecraft following his Mercury and Gemini flight and is the first Astronaut to be brought aboard recovery ships twice in this manner. With him on Gemini 6, was Astronaut Thomas P. Strafford.

He was the Command Pilot on Apollo VII, the first manned flight test of the three direction United States spacecraft. Apollo VII began on October 11, 1968, with Command Module Pilot Donn F. Eisele and Lunar Module Pilot Walter Cunningham. Schirra participated in, and executed, maneuvers enabling crew members to perform exercises in transposition and docking and orbit rendezvous with the S-IVB stage from the Saturn IB launch vehicle. The mission completed eight successful tests and maneuvering ignitions of the service module propulsion engine, measured the accuracy of performance of all spacecraft systems, and provided the first effective television transmission of on-board crew activities. Apollo VII was placed in an orbit with an apogee of 153.5 nautical miles and a perigee of 122.6 nautical miles.

The 260 hours 4.5 million mile shake down flight was concluded on October 22, with splashdown occurring in the Atlantic some 8 miles from the carrier Essex (only 3/10 of a mile from the originally predicted aiming point). Captain Schirra has logged a total of 295 hours and 15 minutes in space. He is unique in that he is the only Astronaut to have flown Mercury, Gemini, and Apollo.

Alan B. Shepard Jr.: Original Mercury 7 Astronaut

PERSONAL DATA: Born November 18, 1923, in East Derry, New Hampshire. He died on July 21, 1998. He was married and had three daughters and six grandchildren.

EDUCATION: Attended primary and secondary schools in East Derry and Derry, New Hampshire; received a Bachelor of Science degree from the United States Naval Academy in 1944, an Honorary Master of Arts degree from Dartmouth College in 1962, and Honorary Doctorate of Science from Miami University (oxford, Ohio) in 1971, and an Honorary Doctorate of Humanities from Franklin Pierce College in 1972. He graduated Naval Test Pilot School in1951; Naval War College, Newport, Rhode Island in 1957.

SPECIAL HONORS; Congressional Medal of Honor (Space): Awarded two NASA Distinguished Service Medals, the NASA Exceptional Service Medal, the Navy Astronaut Wings, the Navy Distinguished Service Medal, and the Navy Distinguished Flying Cross; recipient of the Langley Trophy, the Kinchloe Trophy, the Cabot Award, the Collier Trophy, the City of New York Gold Medal (1971), Achievement Award for 1971. Shepard was appointed by the President in July 1971 as a delegated to the 26th United Nations General Assembly and served through the entire assembly which lasted from September to December 1971.

NASA EXPERIENCE: Rear Admiral Shepard was one of the Mercury astronauts named by NASA in April 1959, and he holds the distinction of being the first American to journey into space. On May 5, 1961, in the freedom 7 spacecraft, he was launched by a Redstone vehicle on a ballistic trajectory suborbital flight-a flight which carried him to an altitude of 116 statute miles and to a landing point 302 statute miles down the Atlantic Missile Range.

In 1963, he was designated Chief of the Astronaut Office with responsibility for monitoring the coordination, scheduling, and control of all activities involving NASA astronauts. This included monitoring the development and implementation of effective training programs to assure the flight readiness of available pilot/non-pilot personnel for assignment to crew positions on manned space flights; furnishing pilot evaluations applicable to the design, construction, and operations of spacecraft systems and related equipment; and providing qualitative scientific and engineering observations to facilitate overall mission planning, formulation of feasible operational procedures, and selection and conduct of specific experiments for each flight.

He was restored to full flight status in May 1969, following corrective surgery for an inner ear disorder.

Shepard made his second space flight as spacecraft commander on Apollo 14, January 31 to February 9, 1971. He was accompanied on man's third lunar landing mission by Stuart A. Roosa, command module, "Antares," to a landing in the hilly upland Fra Mauro region of the moon, Shepard and Mitchell subsequently deployed and activated various scientific equipment and experiments and collected almost 100 pounds of lunar samples for return to earth. Other Apollo 14 achievements included: first use of Mobile Equipment Transporter (MET): largest payload placed in lunar orbit; longest distance traversed on the lunar surface; largest payload returned from the lunar surface; longest lunar surface stay time (33 hours): longest lunar surface EVA (9 hours and 17 minutes): first use of shortened lunar orbit rendezvous techniques; first used of colored TV with new vidicon tube on lunar surface; and first extensive orbital science period conducted during CSM solo operations.

Rear Admiral Shepard has logged a total of 216 hours and 57 minutes in space, of which 9 hours and 17 minutes were spent in lunar surface EVA.

He resumed his duties as Chief of the Astronaut Office in June 1971 and served in this capacity until he retired from NASA and the Navy on August 1, 1974.

THOMAS P. STAFFORD, LIEUTENANT GENERAL, USAF (RET.) NASA ASTRONAUT (FORMER)

PERSONAL DATA: Born September 17, 1930, in Weatherford, Oklahoma. He married to the former Linda Ann Dishman of Chelsea, Oklahoma. They have two sons. First marriage was to the former Faye L. Shoemaker. They have two daughters, as well as two grandsons. Linda has two children from a previous marriage, and four grandchildren.

EDUCATION: Graduated from Weatherford High School, Weatherford, Oklahoma; received a Bachelor of Science degree from the United States Naval Academy in 1952. In addition, General Stafford is the recipient of several honorary degrees. These include a doctorate of laws from the University of Cordoba, Argentina, a doctorate of humane letters, University of Oklahoma and a masters of humane letters, Southwestern University, Weatherford, Oklahoma; a doctorate of science from Oklahoma City University; a doctorate of laws, Western State University, Los Angeles California; doctorate of communications, Emerson College, Boston, Massachusetts; a doctorate of aeronautical engineering, Embry-Riddle Aeronautical University, Daytona Beach, Florida, and a doctorate of humanities, Oklahoma Christian College, Edmond, Oklahoma.

EXPERIENCE: General Strafford was selected among the second group of astronauts in September 1962 by the National Aeronautics and Space Administration (NASA) to participate in Projects Gemini and Apollo. In December

1965, he piloted Gemini VI the first rendezvous in space, and helped develop techniques to prove the basic theory and practicality of space rendezvous. In June 1966 he commanded Gemini IX and performed a demonstration of an early rendezvous that would be used in Apollo, the first optical rendezvous, and a lunar orbit abort rendezvous. From August 1966 to October 1968 he headed the mission planning analysis and software development responsibilities for the astronaut group for Project Apollo.

General Strafford was the lead member of the group, which helped formulate the sequence of missions leading to the first lunar landing mission. He demonstrated and implemented the theory of a pilot manually flying the Saturn booster into orbit and the translunar injection maneuver.

General Strafford was commander of Apollo 10 in May 1969, first flight of the lunar module to the moon, performed the first rendezvous around the moon, and preformed the entire lunar landing mission except the actual landing.

He was also reconnaissance and tracking on future Apollo landing sites. General Strafford was cited in the Guinness Book of World Records for highest speed ever attained by man that occurred during Apollo 10 reentry when the spacecraft attained 24,791 statute miles per hour.

He was assigned as head of the astronaut group in June 1969, responsible for the selection of flight crew for projects Apollo and Skylab. He reviewed and monitored flight crew training status reports, and was responsible for coordination, scheduling, and control of all activities involving NASA astronauts.

In June 1971, General Strafford was assigned as Deputy Director of Flight Crew Operations at the NASA Manned Space flight Center. He was responsible for assisting the director in planning and implementation of programs for the astronaut group, the Aircraft Operations, Flight Crew Integration, Flight Crew Procedures, and Crew Simulation and Training Divisions.

He logged his fourth space flight as Apollo commander of the Apollo-Soyuz Test Project (ASTP) mission, July 15-24, 1975, a joint space flight culminating in the historic first meeting in space between American Astronauts and Soviet Cosmonauts.

Edward Higgins White II, (Lt. Colonel, USAF)

PERSONAL DATA: November 14, 1930, San Antonio, Texas; died January 27, 1967, in the Apollo 204 fire at Cape Kennedy, Florida. Edward Higgins White II was the son of Edward Higgins White, Sr.

EDUCATION: Ed White attended Western High School in Washington, D.C. where he excelled in track as 2nd best hurdler in the area for a time. He received an appointment to West Point where he set the 400-meter hurdles record and nearly made the 1952 Olympics team. He received a Bachelor of Science degree from the U.S. Academy (1952 and master of science in aeronautical engineering from the University of Michigan. 1959).

NASA EXPERIENCE: On September 17, 1962 NASA chose White to be one of the nine out of more than 750 applicants to become an astronaut, in 1962, he was pilot of Gemini 4 (first American to perform extravehicular activity), backup command pilot for Gemini 7, and had been selected to be command module pilot for the first manned Apollo flight. On his EVA flight, Ed White carried a gold cross, a Star of David, and a St. Christopher medal. He commented, "I took these… to express… the faith I had… in the people and the equipment… and… in God." On Friday, January 27, 1967, during a routine test of Apollo One's Spacecraft 012, Ed White Gus Grissom and Roger Chaffee perished in a fire on the launch pad. Ed White would have been among the first three men to launch the Apollo mission to land a man on the moon.

John Young

PERSONAL DATA: Born September 24, 1930, in San Francisco, California. He married to the former Susy Feldman of St. Louis, Missouri. They have two children, two grandchildren.

EDUCATION: Graduated from Orland High School, Orland, Florida; received a Bachelor of Science degree in aeronautical engineering with highest honors from Georgia Institute of Technology in 1952.

NASA EXPERIENCE: In September 1962, Young was selected as an astronaut. He is the 1st person to fly in space 6 times from earth, and 7 times counting his lunar liftoff. The 1st flight was with Gus Grissom in Gemini 3, the 1st manned Gemini mission, on March 23, 1965. This was a complete end-to-end test of the Gemini spacecraft, during which Gus accomplished the 1st manual change of orbit altitude and plane and the 1st lifting reentry, and Young operated the 1st computer on a manned spacecraft. On Gemini 10, July 18-21, 1966, Young, as Commander, and Mike Collins, as Pilot, completed a dual rendezvous with 2 separate Agena target vehicles.

While Young flew close formation on 2nd Agena, Mike Collins did an EVA transfer to retrieve a micro meteorite detector from that Agena. On his 3rd flight, May 18-26, 1969, Young was Command Module of Apollo 10.

Tom Stafford and Gene Cernan were also on this mission which orbited the moon, completed a lunar rendezvous, and tracked proposed lunar landing sites. His 4th space flight, Apollo 16, April 16-27, 1972, was a lunar exploration mission, with Young as Spacecraft Commander, and Ken Mattingly and Charlie Duke. Young and Duke set up scientific equipment and explored the lunar highlands at Descartes. They collected 200 lbs of rocks and drove over 16 miles in the lunar rover on 3 separate geology traverses.

Young was also on 5 backup space flight crews; backup pilot in Gemini 6, backup command module pilot for the second Apollo mission (before the Apollo Program fire) and Apollo 7, and backup spacecraft commander for Apollo 13 and 17. In preparation for prime and backup crew positions on 11 space flights, Young has put more than 15,000 hours into training so far, mostly in simulators and simulations.